21 MINUTES FOR 21 DAYS

A DAILY JOURNEY OF FAITH

FAMILY
Christian Stores

Scripture quotations are taken from:

The Holy Bible, King James Version (KJV)

The Holy Bible, New International Version (NIV) Copyright © 1973, 1978, 1984, by International Bible Society. Used by permission of Zondervan Publishing House. All rights reserved.

The Holy Bible, New King James Version (NKJV) Copyright © 1982 by Thomas Nelson, Inc. Used by permission.

Holy Bible, New Living Translation, (NLT) copyright © 1996. Used by permission of Tyndale House Publishers, Inc., Wheaton, Illinois 60189. All rights reserved.

The Message (MSG)- This edition issued by contractual arrangement with NavPress, a division of The Navigators, U.S.A. Originally published by NavPress in English as THE MESSAGE: The Bible in Contemporary Language copyright 2002-2003 by Eugene Peterson. All rights reserved.

New Century Version®. (NCV) Copyright © 1987, 1988, 1991 by Word Publishing, a division of Thomas Nelson, Inc. All rights reserved. Used by permission.

The New American Standard Bible®, (NASB) Copyright © 1960, 1962, 1963, 1968, 1971, 1972, 1973, 1975, 1977, 1995 by The Lockman Foundation. Used by permission.

The Holman Christian Standard Bible™ (HCSB) Copyright © 1999, 2000, 2001 by Holman Bible Publishers. Used by permission.

Cover Design by Kim Russell / Wahoo Designs
Page Layout by Bart Dawsonn

ISBN 978-1-60587-074-8

Printed in the United States of America

21 MINUTES FOR 21 DAYS

A DAILY JOURNEY OF
FAITH

TABLE OF CONTENTS

INTRODUCTION

If you thought that you could become a more faithful Christian, would you be willing to carve out a few minutes each day for the next three weeks in order to find out? If you answered yes, congratulations! You are about to embark on a grand adventure.

Perhaps you've heard the old saying that it takes 21 days to change a habit. It's a common-sense idea that makes a valid point: if you can do anything for 21 straight days, then there's a very good chance you can keep doing it on the 22nd day and the 23rd and the 24th and beyond.

This book contains 21 chapters, each of which contains a devotional message that are intended to give you courage for today and hope for the future. And each devotional should take no more than 21 minutes to complete.

So here's the big question: Can you spare 21 short minutes a day for God? And can you do so for the next 21 days? Of course you can . . . and of course you should. And make no mistake: when you establish a genuine partnership with the Creator of the universe, you'll be amazed by the things that He and you, working together, can accomplish in 21 short days.

FAITH FOR
THE JOURNEY

For whatever is born of God overcomes the world.
And this is the victory that has
overcome the world—our faith.

1 John 5:4 NKJV

During uncertain times, we may be confronted with an illusion that seems very real indeed: the illusion of hopelessness. Try though we might, we simply can't envision a solution to our problems—and we fall into the darkness of despair. During these times, we may question God—His love, His presence, even His very existence. Despite God's promises, despite Christ's love, and despite our many blessings, we may envision little or no hope for the future. These dark days can be dangerous times for us and for our loved ones.

If you find yourself falling into the spiritual traps of worry and discouragement, seek the encouraging words of fellow Christians and the healing touch of Jesus. After all, it was Christ who promised, "These things I have spoken unto you, that in me ye might have peace. In the world ye shall have tribulation: but be of good cheer; I have overcome the world" (John 16:33 KJV).

Can you place your future into the hands of a loving and all-knowing God? Can you live amid the uncertainties of today, knowing that God has dominion over all your tomorrows? Can you summon the faith to trust God in good times and hard times? If you can, you are wise and you are blessed.

Once you've made the decision to trust God completely, it's time to get busy. The willingness to take action—even if the outcome of that action is uncertain—is an effective way to combat hopelessness. When you decide to roll up your sleeves and begin solving your own problems, you'll feel empowered, and you may see the first real glimmer of hope.

If you're waiting for someone else to solve your problems, or if you're waiting for God to patch things up by Himself, you may become impatient, despondent, or both. But when you stop waiting and start working, God has a way of pitching in and finishing the job. The advice of American publisher Cyrus Curtis still rings true: "Believe in the Lord and He will do half the work—the last half."

So, today and every day, ask God for these things: clear perspective, mountain-moving faith, and the courage to do what needs doing. After all, no problem is too big for God—not even yours.

If I should neglect prayer but a single day,
I should lose a great deal of the fire of faith.
Martin Luther

Faith is seeing light with the eyes of your heart, when the eyes of your body see only darkness.

Barbara Johnson

Joy is faith feasting and celebrating the One in Whom it trusts.

Susan Lenzkes

I want my life to be a faith-filled leap into his arms, knowing he will be there—not that everything will go as I want, but that he will be there and that this will be enough.

Sheila Walsh

If God chooses to remain silent, faith is content.

Ruth Bell Graham

Belief is not the result of an intellectual act; it is the result of an act of my will whereby I deliberately commit myself.

Oswald Chambers

For every mountain there is a miracle.

Robert Schuller

MORE FROM GOD'S WORD ABOUT FAITH

If you do not stand firm in your faith, then you will not stand at all.

Isaiah 7:9 HCSB

Be alert, stand firm in the faith, be brave and strong.

1 Corinthians 16:13 HCSB

For we walk by faith, not by sight.

2 Corinthians 5:7 HCSB

Now faith is the reality of what is hoped for, the proof of what is not seen.

Hebrews 11:1 HCSB

Now without faith it is impossible to please God, for the one who draws near to Him must believe that He exists and rewards those who seek Him.

Hebrews 11:6 HCSB

Faith That Works

Through every stage of your life, God stands by your side, ready to strengthen you and protect you . . . if you have faith in Him. When you place your faith, your trust, indeed your life in the hands of Christ Jesus, you'll be amazed at the marvelous things He can do with you and through you.

So make this promise to yourself and keep it: make certain that your faith is a faith that works. How? You can strengthen your faith through praise, through worship, through Bible study, and through prayer. When you do so, you'll learn to trust God's plans. With Him, all things are possible, and He stands ready to open a world of possibilities to you . . . if you have faith.

Today's Tip

If you don't have faith, you'll never move mountains. But if you do have faith, there's no limit to the things that you and God, working together, can accomplish.

MORE THINGS TO THINK ABOUT

Teach us to set our hopes on heaven, to hold firmly to the promise of eternal life, so that we can withstand the struggles and storms of this world.

Max Lucado

Christ is the only liberator whose liberation lasts forever.

Malcolm Muggeridge

Your choice to either receive or reject the Lord Jesus Christ will determine where you spend eternity.

Anne Graham Lotz

I can still hardly believe it. I, with shriveled, bent fingers, atrophied muscles, gnarled knees, and no feeling from the shoulders down, will one day have a new body— light, bright and clothed in righteousness—powerful and dazzling.

Joni Eareckson Tada

God has promised us abundance, peace, and eternal life. These treasures are ours for the asking; all we must do is claim them. One of the great mysteries of life is why on earth do so many of us wait so very long to lay claim to God's gifts?

Marie T. Freeman

A PRAYER FOR TODAY

Lord, when this world becomes a fearful place,
give me faith. When I am filled with uncertainty
and doubt, give me faith. In the dark moments,
help me to remember that You are always near
and that You can overcome any challenge.
And, in the joyous moments, keep me mindful
that every gift comes from You. In every aspect
of my life, Lord, and in every circumstance,
give me faith. Amen

Today I Will Write Down My Thoughts About . . .

The role that faith plays in my life . . . and the role that faith should play in my life.

_____

_____

_____

_____

_____

_____

_____

_____

_____

_____

_____

_____

_____

_____

_____

_____

_____

THE GIFT OF ETERNAL LIFE

For God so loved the world, that he gave his only begotten Son, that whosoever believeth in him should not perish, but have everlasting life.

John 3:16 KJV

How marvelous it is that God became a man and walked among us. Had He not chosen to do so, we might feel removed from a distant Creator. But ours is not a distant God. Ours is a God who understands—far better than we ever could—the essence of what it means to be human.

God understands our hopes, our fears, and our temptations. He understands what it means to be angry and what it costs to forgive. He knows the heart, the conscience, and the soul of every person who has ever lived, including you. And God has a plan of salvation that is intended for you. Accept it. Accept God's gift through the person of His Son Christ Jesus, and then rest assured: God walked among us so that you might have eternal life; amazing though it may seem, He did it for you.

As mere mortals, our vision for the future, like our lives here on earth, is limited. God's vision is not burdened by such limitations: His plans extend throughout all eternity. Thus, God's plans for you are not limited to the ups and downs of everyday life. Your Heavenly Father has bigger things in mind . . . much bigger things.

Let us praise the Creator for His priceless gift, and let us share the Good News with all who cross our paths. We return our Father's love by accepting His grace and by sharing His message and His love. When we do, we are blessed here on earth and throughout all eternity.

As you struggle through the inevitable hardships and occasional disappointments of life, remember that God has invited you to accept His abundance not only for today but also for all eternity. So keep things in perspective. Although you will inevitably encounter occasional defeats in this world, you'll have all eternity to celebrate the ultimate victory in the next.

And because we know Christ is alive,
we have hope for the present
and hope for life beyond the grave.

Billy Graham

Those of us who know the wonderful grace of redemption look forward to an eternity with God, when all things will be made new, when all our longings will at last find ultimate and final satisfaction.

Joseph Stowell

The damage done to us on this earth will never find its way into that safe city. We can relax, we can rest, and though some of us can hardly imagine it, we can prepare to feel safe and secure for all of eternity.

Bill Hybels

God dwells in eternity, but time dwells in God. He has already lived all our tomorrows as he has lived all our yesterdays.

A. W. Tozer

God did not spring forth from eternity; He brought forth eternity.

C. H. Spurgeon

The choices of time are binding in eternity.

Jack MacArthur

He who has no vision of eternity will never get a true hold of time.

Thomas Carlyle

MORE FROM GOD'S WORD ABOUT ETERNAL LIFE

And this is the will of Him who sent Me, that everyone who sees the Son and believes in Him may have everlasting life; and I will raise him up at the last day.

John 6:40 NKJV

And this is the testimony: that God has given us eternal life, and this life is in His Son. He who has the Son has life; he who does not have the Son of God does not have life.

1 John 5:11-12 NKJV

Don't be troubled. You trust God, now trust in me. There are many rooms in my Father's home, and I am going to prepare a place for you. If this were not so, I would tell you plainly. When everything is ready, I will come and get you, so that you will always be with me where I am.

John 14:1-3 NLT

Pursue righteousness, godliness, faith, love, endurance, and gentleness. Fight the good fight for the faith; take hold of eternal life, to which you were called and have made a good confession before many witnesses.

1 Timothy 6:11-12 HCSB

THIS WORLD IS NOT OUR HOME

Sometimes the troubles of this old world are easier to tolerate when we remind ourselves that heaven is our true home. An old hymn contains the words, "This world is not my home; I'm just passing through." Thank goodness!

This crazy world can be a place of trouble and danger. Thankfully, God has offered you a permanent home in heaven, a place of unimaginable glory, a place that your Heavenly Father has already prepared for you.

In John 16:33, Jesus tells us He has overcome the troubles of this world. We should trust Him, and we should obey His commandments. When we do, we can withstand any problem, knowing that our troubles are temporary, but that heaven is not.

TODAY'S TIP

God offers you a priceless gift: the gift of eternal life. If you have not already done so, accept God's gift today—tomorrow may be too late.

More Things to Think About

Make the least of all that goes and the most of all that comes. Don't regret what is past. Cherish what you have. Look forward to all that is to come. And most important of all, rely moment by moment on Jesus Christ.

Gigi Graham Tchividjian

Hope looks for the good in people, opens doors for people, discovers what can be done to help, lights a candle, does not yield to cynicism. Hope sets people free.

Barbara Johnson

The Christian lifestyle is not one of legalistic do's and don'ts, but one that is positive, attractive, and joyful.

Vonette Bright

Other men see only a hopeless end, but the Christian rejoices in an endless hope.

Gilbert M. Beeken

The popular idea of faith is of a certain obstinate optimism: the hope, tenaciously held in the face of trouble, that the universe is fundamentally friendly and things may get better.

J. I. Packer

A PRAYER FOR TODAY

I know, Lord, that this world is not my home;
I am only here for a brief while.
And, You have given me the priceless gift of
eternal life through Your Son Jesus.
Keep the hope of heaven fresh in my heart,
and, while I am in this world, help me
to pass through it with faith in my heart and
praise on my lips . . . for You. Amen

Today I Will Write Down My Thoughts About . . .

God's promise of eternal life and the nature of my personal relationship with Jesus.

_____

_____

_____

_____

_____

_____

_____

_____

_____

_____

_____

_____

_____

_____

_____

_____

_____

_____

_____

THE POWER OF OPTIMISM

*But if we look forward to something
we don't have yet,
we must wait patiently and confidently.*
Romans 8:25 NLT

Are you a hope-filled, enthusiastic Christian? You should be. After all, as a believer, you have every reason to be optimistic about your life here on earth and your eternal life in heaven. As English clergyman William Ralph Inge observed, "No Christian should be a pessimist, for Christianity is a system of radical optimism." Inge's words are most certainly true, but sometimes, you may find yourself pulled down by the inevitable concerns of everyday life. If you find yourself discouraged, exhausted, or both, then it's time to ask yourself this question: what's bothering you, and why?

If you're overly worried by the inevitable ups and downs of life, God wants to have a little chat with you. After all, God has made promises to you that He intends to keep. And if your life has been transformed by God's only begotten Son, then you, as a recipient of God's grace, have every reason to live courageously.

Are you willing to trust God's plans for your life? Hopefully, you will trust Him completely. After all, the words of the Psalmist make it clear: "The ways of God are without fault. The Lord's words are pure. He is a shield to those who trust him" (Psalm 18:30 NCV). These words should serve as a reminder that even when the challenges of the day seem daunting, God remains steadfast. And, so should you.

So make this promise to yourself and keep it—vow to be an expectant, faith-filled Christian. Think optimistically about your life, your profession, your family, your future, and your purpose for living. Trust your hopes, not your fears. Take time to celebrate God's glorious creation. And then, when you've filled your heart with hope and gladness, share your optimism with others. They'll be better for it, and so will you.

It's your choice:
you can either count your blessings or
recount your disappointments.

Jim Gallery

If you can't tell whether your glass is half-empty or half-full, you don't need another glass; what you need is better eyesight . . . and a more thankful heart.

Marie T. Freeman

Dark as my path may seem to others, I carry a magic light in my heart. Faith, the spiritual strong searchlight, illumines the way, and although sinister doubts lurk in the shadow, I walk unafraid toward the enchanted wood where the foliage is always green, where joy abides, where nightingales nest and sing, and where life and death are one in the presence of the Lord.

Helen Keller

We may run, walk, stumble, drive, or fly, but let us never lose sight of the reason for the journey, or miss a chance to see a rainbow on the way.

Gloria Gaither

The people whom I have seen succeed best in life have always been cheerful and hopeful people who went about their business with a smile on their faces.

Charles Kingsley

There is wisdom in the habit of looking at the bright side of life.

Father Flanagan

MORE FROM GOD'S WORD ABOUT OPTIMISM

Make me hear joy and gladness.

Psalm 51:8 NKJV

My cup runs over. Surely goodness and mercy shall follow me all the days of my life; and I will dwell in the house of the Lord forever.

Psalm 23:5-6 NKJV

I can do everything through him that gives me strength.

Philippians 4:13 NIV

For God has not given us a spirit of fear, but of power and of love and of a sound mind.

2 Timothy 1:7 NLT

Be of good courage, and he shall strengthen your heart, all ye that hope in the LORD.

Psalm 31:24 KJV

Being a Joyful Christian

A joyful life starts with a joyful attitude. So when you're feeling a little tired or sad, here's something to remember: This day is a gift from God. And it's up to you to enjoy this day by trying to be cheerful, helpful, courteous, and well behaved. How can you do these things? A good place to start is by doing your best to think good thoughts.

God wants you to have a happy, joyful life, but that doesn't mean that you'll be happy all the time. Sometimes, you won't feel like feeling happy, and when you don't, you should talk to your friends and family about your emotions. When you talk things over with them, you'll feel better . . . and they'll feel better, too.

Today's Tip

Think about all the things you have (starting with your family and your faith). And think about all the things you can do! If you think you can do something, you probably can. If you think you can't do something, you probably can't. That's why it's so important to believe in yourself.

I could go through this day
oblivious to the miracles
all around me,
or I could tune in and "enjoy."

—

Gloria Gaither

More Things to Think About

Once we recognize our need for Jesus, then the building of our faith begins. It is a daily, moment-by-moment life of absolute dependence upon Him for everything.

Catherine Marshall

When the train goes through a tunnel and the world becomes dark, do you jump out? Of course not. You sit still and trust the engineer to get you through.

Corrie ten Boom

The things we think are the things that feed our souls. If we think on pure and lovely things, we shall grow pure and lovely like them; and the converse is equally true.

Hannah Whitall Smith

I became aware of one very important concept I had missed before: my attitude—not my circumstances—was what was making me unhappy.

Vonette Bright

The life of strain is difficult. The life of inner peace—a life that comes from a positive attitude—is the easiest type of existence.

Norman Vincent Peale

A PRAYER FOR TODAY

Heavenly Father, You love me, You care for me,
and You protect me. You have given me
the priceless gift of eternal life through the
sacrifice that Christ made on the cross
at Calvary. Because of You, Father,
and because of Your Son, I can live each day
with celebration in my heart and praise on
my lips. Let me always be thankful, and let me
share the Good News of Jesus as I turn
my thoughts to You this day and always.
Amen

Today I Will Write Down My Thoughts About . . .

The importance of embracing optimism and the need to reject pessimism.

_____

_____

_____

_____

_____

_____

_____

_____

_____

_____

_____

_____

_____

_____

_____

_____

LEARNING TO TRUST GOD COMPLETELY

Trust in the Lord with all your heart,
and do not rely on your own understanding;
think about Him in all your ways,
and He will guide you on the right paths.
Proverbs 3:5-6 HCSB

The journey through life takes us through many peaks and valleys. When we reach the mountaintops, we find it easy to praise God and to give thanks. As we reach the crest of the mountain's peak, we trust God's plan. But, when we find ourselves in the dark valleys of life, when we face disappointment and despair, it is so much more difficult to trust God. But, trust Him we must.

As Christians, we can be comforted: Whether we find ourselves at the pinnacle of the mountain or the darkest depths of the valley, God is there. And, we Christians have every reason to live courageously. After all, Christ has already won the ultimate battle on the cross at Calvary. Still, even dedicated Christians may find their courage tested by the inevitable disappointments and tragedies that occur in the lives of believers and non-believers alike.

The next time you find your courage tested to the limit, lean upon God's promises. Trust His Son. Remember that God is always near and that He is your protector and your deliverer. When you are worried, anxious, or afraid, call upon Him. God can handle your troubles infinitely better than you can, so turn them over to Him. Remember that God rules both mountaintops and valleys—with limitless wisdom and love—now and forever.

Do not be afraid, then, that if you trust, or tell others to trust, the matter will end there. Trust is only the beginning and the continual foundation. When we trust Him, the Lord works, and His work is the important part of the whole matter.

Hannah Whitall Smith

Brother, is your faith looking upward today? / Trust in the promise of the Savior. / Sister, is the light shining bright on your way? / Trust in the promise of thy Lord.

Fanny Crosby

Sometimes the very essence of faith is trusting God in the midst of things He knows good and well we cannot comprehend.

Beth Moore

Are you serious about wanting God's guidance to become the person he wants you to be? The first step is to tell God that you know you can't manage your own life; that you need his help.

Catherine Marshall

Never be afraid to trust an unknown future to a known God.

Corrie ten Boom

As God's children, we are
the recipients of lavish love—
a love that motivates us to keep
trusting even when we have
no idea what God is doing.

—

Beth Moore

MORE FROM GOD'S WORD ABOUT TRUSTING GOD

Let us hold fast the confession of our hope without wavering, for He who promised is faithful.

Hebrews 10:23 NKJV

For we walk by faith, not by sight.

2 Corinthians 5:7 NKJV

The one who understands a matter finds success, and the one who trusts in the Lord will be happy.

Proverbs 16:20 HCSB

For the eyes of the Lord range throughout the earth to show Himself strong for those whose hearts are completely His.

2 Chronicles 16:9 HCSB

TODAY'S TIP

Trust God? You bet! One of the most important lessons that you can ever learn is to trust God for everything, and that includes timing . . . In other words, you should trust God to decide the best time for things to happen. Sometimes it's hard to trust God, but it's always the right thing to do.

Trusting an All-Powerful Creator

Because God's power is limitless, it is far beyond the comprehension of mortal minds. But even though we cannot fully understand the awesome heart of God, we can praise it, worship it, and marvel at its mercy.

God's ability to love is not burdened by boundaries or by limitations. The love that flows from the awesome heart of God is infinite—and today presents yet another opportunity to celebrate His love.

When we worship God with faith and assurance, and when we place Him at the absolute center of our lives, we invite His love into our hearts. In turn, we grow to love Him more deeply as we sense His love for us. St. Augustine wrote, "I love you, Lord, not doubtingly, but with absolute certainty. Your Word beat upon my heart until I fell in love with you, and now the universe and everything in it tells me to love you." Let us pray that we, too, will turn our hearts to the Creator, knowing with certainty that His awesome heart has ample room for each of us, and that we, in turn, must make room in our hearts for Him.

He granted their request because
they trusted in Him.
1 Chronicles 5:20 HCSB

MORE THINGS TO THINK ABOUT

Christ reigns in His church as shepherd-king. He has supremacy, but it is the superiority of a wise and tender shepherd over His needy and loving flock. He commands and receives obedience, but it is willing obedience of well-cared-for-sheep, offered joyfully to their beloved Shepherd, whose voice they know so well. He rules by the force of love and the energy of goodness.

C. H. Spurgeon

The strength and happiness of a man consists in finding out the way in which God is going, and going that way too.

Henry Ward Beecher

Let your fellowship with the Father and with the Lord Jesus Christ have as its one aim and object a life of quiet, determined, unquestioning obedience.

Andrew Murray

True faith commits us to obedience.

A. W. Tozer

Faith means believing in advance what will only make sense in reverse.

Philip Yancey

A PRAYER FOR TODAY

Dear Lord, I will turn my concerns
over to You. I will trust Your love,
Your wisdom, Your plan, Your promises,
and Your Son—today and every day that I live.
Amen

Today I Will Write Down My Thoughts About . . .

The most important things that I need to ask God today.

_____

_____

_____

_____

_____

_____

_____

_____

_____

_____

_____

_____

_____

_____

_____

_____

_____

_____

OBEDIENCE NOW

Now by this we know that we know Him,
if we keep His commandments.

1 John 2:3 NKJV

God has given us a guidebook for abundant life; that book is the Holy Bible. It contains thorough instructions which, if followed, lead to fulfillment, righteousness and salvation. But, if we choose to ignore God's commandments, the results are as predictable as they are tragic.

How can we demonstrate our love for God? By placing Christ squarely at the center of our lives. Jesus said that if we are to love Him, we must obey His commandments (John 14:15). Thus, our obedience to the Master is an expression of our love for Him.

In Ephesians 2:10 we read, "For we are His workmanship, created in Christ Jesus for good works" (NKJV). These words are instructive: We are not saved by good works, but for good works. Good works are not the root, but rather the fruit of our salvation.

When we seek righteousness in our own lives— and when we seek the companionship of those who do likewise—we reap the spiritual rewards that God intends for our lives. When we behave ourselves as godly people, we honor God. When we live righteously and according to God's commandments, He blesses us in ways that we cannot fully understand.

As families, we should take every step of our journey with God. We should continue to read His Word and we should continue to follow His commandments. We should support only those activities that further God's kingdom and our own spiritual growth. And we should be worthy examples to our friends and neighbors. When we do, we'll reap the blessings that God has promised to all those who live according to His will and His Word.

When the law of God is written on our hearts,
our duty will be our delight.

Matthew Henry

Mary could not have dreamed all that would result from her faithful obedience. Likewise, you cannot possibly imagine all that God has in store for you when you trust him.

Henry Blackaby

Let us never suppose that obedience is impossible or that holiness is meant only for a select few. Our Shepherd leads us in paths of righteousness—not for our name's sake but for His.

Elisabeth Elliot

When you suffer and lose, that does not mean you are being disobedient to God. In fact, it might mean you're right in the center of His will. The path of obedience is often marked by times of suffering and loss.

Charles Swindoll

I don't always like His decisions, but when I choose to obey Him, the act of obedience still "counts" with Him even if I'm not thrilled about it.

Beth Moore

Trials and sufferings teach us to obey the Lord by faith, and we soon learn that obedience pays off in joyful ways.

Bill Bright

MORE FROM GOD'S WORD ABOUT OBEDIENCE

Choose for yourselves today the one you will worship . . . . As for me and my family, we will worship the Lord.

Joshua 24:15 HCSB

Therefore, get your minds ready for action, being self-disciplined, and set your hope completely on the grace to be brought to you at the revelation of Jesus Christ. As obedient children, do not be conformed to the desires of your former ignorance but, as the One who called you is holy, you also are to be holy in all your conduct.

1 Peter 1:13-15 HCSB

But whoever keeps His word, truly the love of God is perfected in him. By this we know that we are in Him. He who says he abides in Him ought himself also to walk just as He walked.

1 John 2:5-6 NKJV

For this is what love for God is: to keep His commands. Now His commands are not a burden, because whatever has been born of God conquers the world. This is the victory that has conquered the world: our faith.

1 John 5:3-4 HCSB

Actions and Beliefs

Our theology must be demonstrated, not only by our words but, more importantly, by our actions. As Christians, we must do our best to make sure that our actions are accurate reflections of our beliefs. In short, we should be practical believers, quick to act whenever we see an opportunity to serve God.

We may proclaim our beliefs to our hearts' content, but our proclamations will mean nothing—to others or to ourselves—unless we accompany our words with deeds that match. The sermons that we live are far more compelling than the ones we preach. So remember this: whether you like it or not, your life is an accurate reflection of your creed. If this fact gives you cause for concern, don't bother talking about the changes that you intend to make— make them. And then, when your good deeds speak for themselves—as they most certainly will—don't interrupt.

Today's Tip

Obedience leads to spiritual growth. Oswald Chambers correctly observed, "We grow spiritually as our Lord grew physically: by a life of simple, unobtrusive obedience." When you take these words to heart, you will embark upon a lifetime of spiritual growth . . . and God will smile.

More Things to Think About

Christians are the citizens of heaven, and while we are on earth, we ought to behave like heaven's citizens.

Warren Wiersbe

Life is a series of choices between the bad, the good, and the best. Everything depends on how we choose.

Vance Havner

Order your soul; reduce your wants; associate in Christian community; obey the laws; trust in Providence

St. Augustine

He leads us in the paths of righteousness wherever we are placed.

Oswald Chambers

Although God causes all things to work together for good for His children, He still holds us accountable for our behavior.

Kay Arthur

Discrepancies between values and practices create chaos in a person's life.

John Maxwell

A PRAYER FOR TODAY

Dear Lord, today, I will choose to please You
and only You. I will obey Your commandments,
and I will praise You for Your gifts,
for Your love, and for Your Son. Amen

Today I Will Write Down My Thoughts About . . .

The wisdom of being obedient to God.

_____

_____

_____

_____

_____

_____

_____

_____

_____

_____

_____

_____

_____

_____

_____

_____

_____

THE POWER OF PRAYER

And everything—whatever you ask in prayer,
believing—you will receive.
Matthew 21:22 HCSB

Does prayer play an important role in the life of your family? Is prayer an integral part of your daily routine, or is it a hit-or-miss activity? Do you "pray without ceasing," or is your prayer life an afterthought? If you genuinely wish to receive that abundance that is available through Christ, you must pray constantly, and you must never underestimate the power of prayer.

As you contemplate the quality of your family's prayer life, here are a few things to consider: 1. God hears our prayers and answers them (Jeremiah 29:11-12). 2. God promises that the prayers of righteous people can accomplish great things (James 5:16). 3. God invites us to be still and to feel His presence (Psalm 46:10).

So pray. Pray as a family and pray individually. Start praying in the early morning and keep praying until you fall off to sleep at night. Pray about matters great and small and be watchful for the answers that God most assuredly sends your way.

Daily prayer and meditation is a matter of will and habit. When you organize your day to include quiet moments with God, you'll soon discover that no time is more precious than the silent moments you spend with Him.

The quality of your spiritual life will be in direct proportion to the quality of your prayer life. So do yourself and your loved ones a favor: instead of turning things over in your mind, turn them over to God in prayer. Instead of worrying about your next decision, ask God to lead the way. Don't limit your prayers to meals or to bedtime. Pray constantly because God is listening—and He wants to hear from you. And without question, you need to hear from Him.

Allow your dreams a place in your prayers and plans. God-given dreams can help you move into the future He is preparing for you.

Barbara Johnson

Prayer guards hearts and minds and causes God to bring peace out of chaos.

Beth Moore

Those who know God the best are the richest and most powerful in prayer. Little acquaintance with God, and strangeness and coldness to Him, make prayer a rare and feeble thing.

E. M. Bounds

My soul, hearken to the voice of your God. He is always ready to speak with you when you are prepared to hear. If there is any slowness to commune, it is not on His part but altogether on your own. He stands at the door and knocks, and if His people will only open, He rejoices to enter.

C. H. Spurgeon

God delights in the prayers of His children—prayers that express our love for Him, prayers that share our deepest burdens with Him.

Billy Graham

When we feel like the prey, a victim of evil pursuit, it's time for us to pray and take action against our predator.

Serita Ann Jakes

Pour out your heart to God and tell Him how you feel. Be real, be honest, and when you get it all out, you'll start to feel the gradual covering of God's comforting presence.

Bill Hybels

Don't be overwhelmed . . . take it one day and one prayer at a time.

Stormie Omartian

The manifold rewards of a serious, consistent prayer life demonstrate clearly that time with our Lord should be our first priority.

Shirley Dobson

The center of power is not to be found in summit meetings or in peace conferences. It is not in Peking or Washington or the United Nations, but rather where a child of God prays in the power of the Spirit for God's will to be done in her life, in her home, and in the world around her.

Ruth Bell Graham

Two wings are necessary to lift our souls toward God: prayer and praise. Prayer asks. Praise accepts the answer.

Mrs. Charles E. Cowman

The Power of Prayer

"The power of prayer": these words are so familiar, yet sometimes we forget what they mean. Prayer is a unique tool for communicating with our Creator; it is an opportunity to commune with the Giver of all things good. Prayer is not a thing to be taken lightly or to be used infrequently.

All too often, amid the rush of daily life, we may lose sight of God's presence in our lives. Instead of turning to Him for guidance and for comfort, we depend, instead, upon our own resources. To do so is a profound mistake. Prayer should never be reserved for mealtimes or for bedtimes; it should be an ever-present focus in our daily lives.

Rejoice always! Pray constantly. Give thanks in everything, for this is God's will for you in Christ Jesus.

Today's Tip

When you've got a choice to make, pray about it—one way to make sure that your heart is in tune with God is to pray often. The more you talk to God, the more He will talk to you.

MORE THINGS TO THINK ABOUT

It is well said that neglected prayer is the birth-place of all evil.

C. H. Spurgeon

Obedience is the master key to effective prayer.

Billy Graham

The Christian on his knees sees more than the philosopher on tiptoe.

D. L. Moody

On our knees we are the most powerful force on earth.

Billy Graham

Jesus likes us to vocalize our needs.

Liz Curtis Higgs

Learn to pray to God in such a way that you are trusting Him as your Physician to do what He knows is best. Confess to Him the disease, and let Him choose the remedy.

St. Augustine

The Lord desires a personal, two-way conversation with each of us.

Shirley Dobson

A PRAYER FOR TODAY

Dear Lord, I will open my heart to You.
I will take my concerns, my fears, my plans,
and my hopes to You in prayer. And, then,
I will trust the answers that You give.
You are my loving Father, and I will accept
Your will for my life today and
every day that I live. Amen

Today I Will Write Down My Thoughts About . . .

The role that prayer currently plays in my life, and the role
that it should play.

_____

_____

_____

_____

_____

_____

_____

_____

_____

_____

_____

_____

_____

_____

_____

_____

_____

A FAITH THAT'S BIGGER THAN FEAR

Be strong and courageous, and do the work.
Don't be afraid or discouraged by the size of the task,
for the LORD God, my God, is with you.
He will not fail you or forsake you.

1 Chronicles 28:20 NLT

Every person's life is a tapestry of events: some wonderful, some not-so-wonderful, and some downright disastrous. When we visit the mountaintops of life, praising God isn't hard—in fact, it's easy. In our moments of triumph, we can bow our heads and thank God for our victories. But when we fail to reach the mountaintops, when we endure the inevitable losses that are a part of every person's life, we find it much tougher to give God the praise He deserves. Yet wherever we find ourselves, whether on the mountaintops of life or in life's darkest valleys, we must still offer thanks to God, giving thanks in all circumstances.

When you form a genuine one-on-one relationship with God, you can be comforted by the fact that wherever you find yourself, whether at the top of the mountain or the depths of the valley, God is there with you. And because your Creator cares for you and protects you, you can live courageously.

If you genuinely trust God's Word and believe it, you have every reason to live courageously. After all, the ultimate battle—and your ultimate salvation—has already been won on the cross at Calvary. But sometimes, even if you're a faithful servant and a dedicated follower of the Man from Galilee, you're going to have your courage tested by the inevitable disappointments and fears that visit the lives of believers and non-believers alike.

When you find yourself worried about the challenges of today or the uncertainties of tomorrow, you'll need to ask yourself this question: are you really ready to place your concerns and your life in God's all-powerful, all-knowing, all-loving hands? If the answer to that question is yes—as it should be—then you can draw courage today from the source of strength that never fails: your Father in heaven.

God is not a distant being. He is not absent from our world, nor is He absent from your world. God is not "out there"; He is "right here," continuously reshaping His universe, and continuously reshaping the lives of those who dwell in it.

God is with you always, listening to your thoughts and prayers, watching over your every move. If the demands of everyday life weigh down upon you, you may be tempted to ignore God's presence or—worse yet—to lose faith in His promises. But, when you quiet yourself and acknowledge His presence, God will touch your heart and restore your courage.

At this very moment—as you're fulfilling your obligations—God is seeking to work in you and through you. He's asking you to live abundantly and courageously . . . and He's ready to help. So why not let Him do it . . . starting now?

Courage is almost a contradiction in terms. It means a strong desire to live taking the form of a readiness to die.

G. K. Chesterton

God did away with all my fear. It was time for someone to stand up—or in my case, sit down. So I refused to move.

Rosa Parks

Jesus Christ can make the weakest man into a divine dreadnought, fearing nothing.

Oswald Chambers

A man who is intimate with God will never be intimidated by men.

Leonard Ravenhill

There comes a time when we simply have to face the challenges in our lives and stop backing down.

John Eldredge

When once we are assured that God is good, then there can be nothing left to fear.

Hannah Whitall Smith

MORE FROM GOD'S WORD ABOUT COURAGE

Therefore, being always of good courage . . . we walk by faith, not by sight.

2 Corinthians 5:6-7 NASB

God doesn't want us to be shy with his gifts, but bold and loving and sensible.

2 Timothy 1:7 MSG

The LORD himself goes before you and will be with you; he will never leave you nor forsake you. Do not be afraid; do not be discouraged.

Deuteronomy 31:8 NIV

But Moses said to the people, "Do not fear! Stand by and see the salvation of the LORD."

Exodus 14:13 NASB

So do not fear, for I am with you; do not be dismayed, for I am your God. I will strengthen you and help you; I will uphold you with my righteous right hand.

Isaiah 41:10 NIV

A Strength That Never Fails

When you find yourself worried about the challenges of today or the uncertainties of tomorrow, you must ask yourself whether or not you are ready to place your concerns and your life in God's all-powerful, all-knowing, all-loving hands. If the answer to that question is yes—as it should be—then you can draw courage today from the source of strength that never fails: your Father in heaven.

Even when Old Man Trouble arrives at your doorstep for an extended stay, you can find comfort and courage in the certain knowledge that your Creator is acutely aware of your pain, and that He is perfectly willing and perfectly able to heal your broken heart.

So when tough times arrive, depend upon friends and family members, of course. But also depend upon God. He is trustworthy, now and forever, amen.

Today's Tip

With God as your partner, you have nothing to fear. Why? Because you and God, working together, can handle absolutely anything that comes your way. So the next time you'd like an extra measure of courage, recommit yourself to a true one-on-one relationship with your Creator. When you sincerely turn to Him, He will never fail you.

MORE THINGS TO THINK ABOUT

If a person fears God, he or she has no reason to fear anything else. On the other hand, if a person does not fear God, then fear becomes a way of life.

Beth Moore

With each new experience of letting God be in control, we gain courage and reinforcement for daring to do it again and again.

Gloria Gaither

Are you fearful? First, bow your head and pray for God's strength. Then, raise your head knowing that, together, you and God can handle whatever comes your way.

Jim Gallery

Dreaming the dream of God is not for cowards.

Joey Johnson

What is courage? It is the ability to be strong in trust, in conviction, in obedience. To be courageous is to step out in faith—to trust and obey, no matter what.

Kay Arthur

Fill your mind with thoughts of God rather than thoughts of fear.

Norman Vincent Peale

A PRAYER FOR TODAY

Dear Lord, sometimes I face challenges that
leave me worried and afraid. When I am fearful,
let me seek Your strength. When I am anxious,
give me faith. Keep me mindful, Lord, that You
are my God. With You by my side, Lord,
I have nothing to fear today, tomorrow,
or forever. Amen

Today I Will Write Down My Thoughts About . . .

The strength and courage I can draw from God.

_____

_____

_____

_____

_____

_____

_____

_____

_____

_____

_____

_____

_____

_____

_____

_____

_____

_____

DISCOVERING GOD'S PEACE

I leave you peace; my peace I give you.
I do not give it to you as the world does.
So don't let your hearts be troubled or afraid.

John 14:27 NCV

Have you found the lasting peace that can—and should—be yours through Jesus Christ? Or are you still chasing the illusion of "peace and happiness" that the world promises but cannot deliver?

The beautiful words of John 14:27 promise that Jesus offers peace, not as the world gives, but as He alone gives. Your challenge is to accept Christ's peace and then, as best you can, to share His peace with your neighbors. But sometimes, that's easier said than done.

If you are a person with lots of obligations and plenty of responsibilities, it is simply a fact of life: You worry. From time to time, you worry about finances, safety, health, home, family, or about countless other concerns, some great and some small. Where is the best place to take your worries? Take them to God . . . and leave them there.

The Scottish preacher George McDonald observed, "It has been well said that no man ever sank under the burden of the day. It is when tomorrow's burden is added to the burden of today that the weight is more than a man can bear. Never load yourselves so, my friends. If you find yourselves so loaded, at least remember this: it is your own doing, not God's. He begs you to leave the future to Him."

Today, as a gift to yourself, to your family, and to your friends, claim the inner peace that is your spiritual birthright: the peace of Jesus Christ. Christ is standing at the door, waiting patiently for you to invite Him to reign over your heart. His eternal peace is offered freely. Claim it today.

We're prone to want God to change
our circumstances,
but He wants to change our character.
We think that peace comes from the outside in,
but it comes from the inside out.

Warren Wiersbe

The Christian has a deep, silent, hidden peace, which the world sees not, like some well in a retired and shady place.

John Henry Cardinal Newman

That peace, which has been described and which believers enjoy, is a participation of the peace which their glorious Lord and Master himself enjoys.

Jonathan Edwards

There may be no trumpet sound or loud applause when we make a right decision, just a calm sense of resolution and peace.

Gloria Gaither

We need to be at peace with our past, content with our present, and sure about our future, knowing they are all in God's hands.

Joyce Meyer

Peace and love are always alive in us, but we are not always alive to peace and love.

Juliana of Norwich

God has revealed to us a new reality that the world does not understand: In his eternal kingdom, what matters is being like our Father. That is the way to success and peace.

Mary Morrison Suggs

MORE FROM GOD'S WORD ABOUT

If your sinful nature controls your mind, there is death. But if the Holy Spirit controls your mind, there is life and peace.

Romans 8:6 NLT

If it is possible, as far as it depends on you, live at peace with everyone.

Romans 12:18 NIV

Live peaceful and quiet lives in all godliness and holiness.

1 Timothy 2:2 NIV

TODAY'S TIP

Whatever it is, God can handle it: Sometimes peace is a scarce commodity in a demanding, 21st-century world. How can we find the peace that we so desperately desire? By turning our days and our lives over to God. Elisabeth Elliot writes, "If my life is surrendered to God, all is well. Let me not grab it back, as though it were in peril in His hand but would be safer in mine!" May we give our lives, our hopes, and our prayers to the Father, and, by doing so, accept His will and His peace.

Peace Today and Forever

On many occasions, our outer struggles are simply manifestations of the inner conflicts that we feel when we stray from God's path. What's needed is a refresher course in God's promise of peace.

The words of Psalm 119:165 remind us that God offers peace to those who accept His instruction. Count yourself among that number. Study God's promises carefully and trust them completely. When you do, you will be a beacon of wisdom to your family and to your world.

So don't focus too intently on the inevitable distractions and frustrations of everyday living. Instead, be still and invite God to preside over every aspect of your life. It's the best way to live and the surest path to peace . . . today and forever.

Blessed are the peacemakers,
for they will be called sons of God.
Matthew 5:9 NIV

The better acquainted
you become with God,
the less tensions you feel and
the more peace you possess.

—

Charles Allen

MORE THINGS TO THINK ABOUT

When we do what is right, we have contentment, peace, and happiness.

Beverly LaHaye

Look around you and you'll be distressed; look within yourself and you'll be depressed; look at Jesus, and you'll be at rest!

Corrie ten Boom

A great many people are trying to make peace, but that has already been done. God has not left it for us to do; all we have to do is to enter into it.

D. L. Moody

Peace comes only when we acknowledge that human effort cannot sustain righteousness any more than it could create it.

Susan Lenzkes

Let's please God by actively seeking, through prayer, "peaceful and quiet lives" for ourselves, our spouses, our children and grandchildren, our friends, and our nation (1 Timothy 2:1-3 NIV).

Shirley Dobson

A PRAYER FOR TODAY

The world talks about peace, but only You,
Lord, can give a perfect and lasting peace.
True peace comes through the Prince of Peace,
and His peace passes all understanding.
Help me to accept His peace—and share it—
this day and forever. Amen

Today I Will Write Down My Thoughts About . . .

Whether or not I'm really experiencing the genuine peace that can and should be mine through Jesus.

_____

_____

_____

_____

_____

_____

_____

_____

_____

_____

_____

_____

_____

_____

_____

_____

_____

THE JOURNEY TOWARD SPIRITUAL MATURITY

For this reason we also, since the day we heard it,
do not cease to pray for you,
and to ask that you may be filled with
the knowledge of His will in all wisdom
and spiritual understanding.

Colossians 1:9 NKJV

The path to spiritual maturity unfolds day by day. Each day offers the opportunity to worship God, to ignore God, or to rebel against God. When we worship Him with our prayers, our words, our thoughts, and our actions, we are blessed by the richness of our relationship with the Father. But if we ignore God altogether or intentionally rebel against His commandments, we rob ourselves of His blessings.

If we study God's Word, if we obey His commandments, and if we live in the center of His will, we will not be "stagnant" believers; we will, instead, be growing Christians . . . and that's exactly what God wants for our lives.

Many of life's most important lessons are painful to learn, but spiritual growth need not take place only in times of adversity. We must seek to grow in our knowledge and love of the Lord in every season of life. Thankfully, God always stands at the door; whenever we are ready to reach out to Him, He will answer.

In those quiet moments when we open our hearts to the Father, the One who made us keeps remaking us. He gives us direction, perspective, wisdom, and courage. And, the appropriate moment to accept those spiritual gifts is always the present one.

Are you as mature as you're ever going to be? Hopefully not! When it comes to your faith, God doesn't intend for you to become "fully grown," at least not in this lifetime. In fact, God still has important lessons that He intends to teach you. So ask yourself this: what lesson is God trying to teach me today? And then go about the business of learning it.

Be patient. God is using today's difficulties
to strengthen you for tomorrow.
He is equipping you.
The God who makes things grow
will help you bear fruit.

Max Lucado

Don't go through life, grow through life.

Eric Butterworth

Growth takes place in quietness, in hidden ways, in silence and solitude. The process is not accessible to observation.

Eugene Peterson

We often become mentally and spiritually barren because we're so busy.

Franklin Graham

God is teaching me to become more and more "teachable": To keep evolving. To keep taking the risk of learning something new . . . or unlearning something old and off base.

Beth Moore

Recently I've been learning that life comes down to this: God is in everything. Regardless of what difficulties I am experiencing at the moment, or what things aren't as I would like them to be, I look at the circumstances and say, "Lord, what are you trying to teach me?"

Catherine Marshall

If I long to improve my brother, the first step toward doing so is to improve myself.

Christina Rossetti

MORE FROM GOD'S WORD ABOUT
SPIRITUAL GROWTH

So let us stop going over the basics of Christianity again and again. Let us go on instead and become mature in our understanding.

Hebrews 6:1 NLT

Run away from infantile indulgence. Run after mature righteousness—faith, love, peace—joining those who are in honest and serious prayer before God.

2 Timothy 2:22 MSG

For You, O God, have tested us; You have refined us as silver is refined. You brought us into the net; You laid affliction on our backs. You have caused men to ride over our heads; we went through fire and through water; but You brought us out to rich fulfillment.

Psalm 66:10–12 NKJV

Know the love of Christ which surpasses knowledge, that you may be filled up to all the fullness of God.

Ephesians 3:19 NASB

ENDURANCE LEADS TO SPIRITUAL MATURITY

From time to time, all of us encounter circumstances that test our faith. When we encounter life's inevitable tragedies, trials, and disappointments, we may be tempted to blame God or to rebel against Him. But these verses remind us that the trials of life can and should be viewed as tools through which we become "mature and complete, lacking nothing."

Have you recently encountered one of life's inevitable tests? If so, remember that God still has lessons that He intends to teach you. So ask yourself this: what lesson is God trying to teach me today?

TODAY'S TIP

Growing to spiritual maturity requires a plan. What is yours? And while you're thinking about the answer to that question, remember this: Spiritual maturity is a journey, not a destination—and a growing relationship with God should be your highest priority.

MORE THINGS TO THINK ABOUT

The whole idea of belonging to Christ is to look less and less like we used to and more and more like Him.

Angela Thomas

As I have continued to grow in my Christian maturity, I have discovered that the Holy Spirit does not let me get by with anything.

Anne Graham Lotz

Grace meets you where you are, but it doesn't leave you where it found you.

Anne Lamott

The vigor of our spiritual lives will be in exact proportion to the place held by the Bible in our lives and in our thoughts.

George Mueller

In reading the Bible, we study to know God, to hear his voice, and to be changed by him as we grow in holiness.

James Montgomery Boice

God loves us the way we are, but He loves us too much to leave us that way.

Leighton Ford

A PRAYER FOR TODAY

Dear Lord, the Bible tells me that You
are at work in my life, continuing to help me
grow and to mature in my faith. Show me
Your wisdom, Father, and let me live according
to Your Word and Your will. Amen

Today I Will Write Down My Thoughts About . . .

Ways that I can continue to grow spiritually and emotionally.

_____

_____

_____

_____

_____

_____

_____

_____

_____

_____

_____

_____

_____

_____

_____

ASKING GOD FOR THE THINGS YOU NEED

So I say to you, ask, and it will be given to you; seek, and you will find; knock, and it will be opened to you. For everyone who asks receives, and he who seeks finds, and to him who knocks it will be opened.

Luke 11:9-10 NKJV

How often do you ask God for His help and His wisdom? Occasionally? Intermittently? Whenever you experience a crisis? Hopefully not. Hopefully, you've acquired the habit of asking for God's assistance early and often. And hopefully, you have learned to seek His guidance in every aspect of your life.

Jesus made it clear to His disciples: they should petition God to meet their needs. So should you. Genuine, heartfelt prayer produces powerful changes in you and in your world. When you lift your heart to God, you open yourself to a never-ending source of divine wisdom and infinite love.

James 5:16 makes a promise that God intends to keep: when you pray earnestly, fervently, and often, great things will happen. Too many people, however, are too timid or too pessimistic to ask God to do big things. Please don't count yourself among their number.

God can do great things through you if you have the courage to ask Him (and the determination to keep asking Him). But don't expect Him to do all the work. When you do your part, He will do His part—and when He does, you can expect miracles to happen.

The Bible promises that God will guide you if you let Him. Your job is to let Him. But sometimes, you will be tempted to do otherwise. Sometimes, you'll be tempted to go along with the crowd; other times, you'll be tempted to do things your way, not God's way. When you feel those temptations, resist them.

God has promised that when you ask for His help, He will not withhold it. So ask. Ask Him to meet the needs of your day. Ask Him to lead you, to protect you, and to correct you. Then, trust the answers He gives.

God stands at the door and waits. When you knock, He opens. When you ask, He answers. Your task, of course, is to make God a full partner in every aspect of your life— and to seek His guidance prayerfully, confidently, and often.

We get into trouble when we think
we know what to do and
we stop asking God if we're doing it.

Stormie Omartian

All we have to do is to acknowledge our need, move from self-sufficiency to dependence, and ask God to become our hiding place.

                                                    Bill Hybels

Some people think God does not like to be troubled with our constant asking. But, the way to trouble God is not to come at all.

                                                    D. L. Moody

Notice that we must ask. And we will sometimes struggle to hear and struggle with what we hear. But personally, it's worth it. I'm after the path of life—and he alone knows it.

                                                    John Eldredge

Don't be afraid to ask your heavenly Father for anything you need. Indeed, nothing is too small for God's attention or too great for his power.

                                                    Dennis Swanberg

When will we realize that we're not troubling God with our questions and concerns? His heart is open to hear us— his touch nearer than our next thought—as if no one in the world existed but us. Our very personal God wants to hear from us personally.

                                                    Gigi Graham Tchividjian

More from God's Word About Asking God

From now on, whatever you request along the lines of who I am and what I am doing, I'll do it. That's how the Father will be seen for who he is in the Son. I mean it. Whatever you request in this way, I'll do.

John 14:13-14 MSG

You did not choose me, but I chose you and appointed you to go and bear fruit—fruit that will last. Then the Father will give you whatever you ask in my name.

John 15:16 NIV

You fathers—if your children ask for a fish, do you give them a snake instead? Or if they ask for an egg, do you give them a scorpion? Of course not! If you sinful people know how to give good gifts to your children, how much more will your heavenly Father give the Holy Spirit to those who ask him.

Luke 11:11-13 NLT

Do not worry about anything, but pray and ask God for everything you need, always giving thanks.

Philippians 4:6 NCV

You do not have, because you do not ask God.

James 4:2 NIV

MOUNTAIN MOVING

God offers us priceless gifts, and we should accept them—but oftentimes, we don't. Why? Because we fail to trust our Heavenly Father completely, and because we are, at times, surprisingly inflexible. Luke 11 teaches us that God does not withhold spiritual gifts from those who ask. Our obligation, quite simply, is to ask for those gifts.

Are you asking God to move mountains in your life? Do you expect God to help you achieve the peace that He has promised? Are you comfortable with the direction of your future? If you need help, of whatever kind, God can give it.

Whatever the size of your challenges, God is ready and willing to help you solve them. So ask for His help today, with faith and with fervor, and then watch in amazement as your mountains begin to move.

TODAY'S TIP

Today, think of a specific need that is weighing heavily on your heart. Then, spend a few quiet moments asking God for His guidance and for His help.

More Things to Think About

When you ask God to do something, don't ask timidly; put your whole heart into it.

Marie T. Freeman

God's help is always available, but it is only given to those who seek it.

Max Lucado

It is our part to seek, His to grant what we ask; our part to make a beginning, His to bring it to completion; our part to offer what we can, His to finish what we cannot.

St. Jerome

We honor God by asking for great things when they are a part of His promise. We dishonor Him and cheat ourselves when we ask for molehills where He has promised mountains.

Vance Havner

If we do not have hearts that call out to him, we forfeit the deliverance. "You do not have, because you do not ask God" (James 4:2 NIV) is probably the saddest commentary on any life, especially the life of a Christian.

Jim Cymbala

A PRAYER FOR TODAY

Lord, today I will ask You for the things
I need. In every situation, I will come to You in
prayer. You know what I want, Lord, and more
importantly, You know what I need.
Yet even though I know that You know,
I still won't be too timid—or too busy—to ask.
Amen

Today I Will Write Down My Thoughts About . . .

The things that I need to ask God today.

_____

_____

_____

_____

_____

_____

_____

_____

_____

_____

_____

_____

_____

_____

_____

_____

_____

_____

_____

ABOVE AND BEYOND OUR WORRIES

Come to Me, all you who labor and are heavy laden, and I will give you rest. Take My yoke upon you and learn from Me, for I am gentle and lowly in heart, and you will find rest for your souls. For My yoke is easy and My burden is light.

Matthew 11:28-30 NKJV

Because you have the ability to think, you also have the ability to worry. Even if you're a very faithful Christian, you may be plagued by occasional periods of discouragement and doubt. Even though you trust God's promise of salvation—even though you sincerely believe in God's love and protection—you may find yourself upset by the countless details of everyday life. Jesus understood your concerns when He spoke the reassuring words found in the 6th chapter of Matthew.

Therefore I say to you, do not worry about your life, what you will eat or what you will drink; nor about your body, what you will put on. Is not life more than food and the body more than clothing? Look at the birds of the air, for they neither sow nor reap nor gather into barns; yet your heavenly Father feeds them. Are you not of more value than they? Which of you by worrying can add one cubit to his stature? . . . Therefore do not worry about tomorrow, for tomorrow will worry about its own things. Sufficient for the day is its own trouble. (vv. 25-27, 34 NKJV)

Where is the best place to take your worries? Take them to God. Take your troubles to Him; take your fears to Him; take your doubts to Him; take your weaknesses to Him; take your sorrows to Him . . . and leave them all there. Seek protection from the One who offers you eternal salvation; build your spiritual house upon the Rock that cannot be moved.

Perhaps you are concerned about your future, your relationships, or your finances. Or perhaps you are simply a "worrier" by nature. If so, choose to make Matthew 6 a regular part of your daily Bible reading. This beautiful passage will remind you that God still sits in His heaven and you are His beloved child. Then, perhaps, you will worry a little less and trust God a little more, and that's as it should be because God is trustworthy . . . and you are protected.

I've read the last page of the Bible.
It's all going to turn out all right.

Billy Graham

Worry is a complete waste of energy. It solves nothing. And it won't solve that anxiety on your mind either.

Charles Swindoll

Worry is the senseless process of cluttering up tomorrow's opportunities with leftover problems from today.

Barbara Johnson

It has been well said that no man ever sank under the burden of the day. It is when tomorrow's burden is added to the burden of today that the weight is more than a man can bear. Never load yourselves so, my friends. If you find yourselves so loaded, at least remember this: it is your own doing, not God's. He begs you to leave the future to Him and mind the present.

George MacDonald

We are not called to be burden-bearers, but cross-bearers and light-bearers. We must cast our burdens on the Lord.

Corrie ten Boom

Never yield to gloomy anticipation. Place your hope and confidence in God. He has no record of failure.

Mrs. Charles E. Cowman

MORE FROM GOD'S WORD ABOUT WORRY

I was very worried, but you comforted me . . . .

Psalm 94:19 NCV

An anxious heart weighs a man down . . . .

Proverbs 12:25 NIV

Don't fret or worry. Instead of worrying, pray. Let petitions and praises shape your worries into prayers, letting God know your concerns. Before you know it, a sense of God's wholeness, everything coming together for good, will come and settle you down. It's wonderful what happens when Christ displaces worry at the center of your life.

Philippians 4:6-7 MSG

Jesus said, "Don't let your hearts be troubled. Trust in God, and trust in me."

John 14:1 NCV

He will wipe away every tear from their eyes. Death will exist no longer; grief, crying, and pain will exist no longer, because the previous things have passed away.

Revelation 21:4 HCSB

No Worries

In the game of life, you win some, and you lose some. Life is risky business; you live in an uncertain world, a world in which trouble may come calling at any moment. No wonder you may find yourself feeling a little panicky at times.

Do you sometimes spend more time worrying about a problem than you spend solving it? If so, remember this strategy for dealing with your worries: Take them to God. Take your troubles to Him; take your fears to Him; take your doubts to Him; take your weaknesses to Him; take your sorrows to Him . . . and leave them all there. Period.

God is the Rock that cannot be moved. When you build your life upon that Rock, you have absolutely no need to worry . . . not now, not ever.

Today's Tip

If you're worried about the future . . . stop worrying and start working. The more time you spend working, the less time you'll have to spend worrying. Don't fret about your problems; fix them!

The beginning of anxiety is
the end of faith,
and the beginning of true faith is
the end of anxiety.

—

George Mueller

MORE THINGS TO THINK ABOUT

God is great; God is good; God loves you, and He sent His Son to die for your sins. When you keep these things in mind, you'll discover that it's hard to stay worried for long.

Marie T. Freeman

He treats us as sons, and all He asks in return is that we shall treat Him as a Father whom we can trust without anxiety. We must take the son's place of dependence and trust, and we must let Him keep the father's place of care and responsibility.

Hannah Whitall Smith

Worry and anxiety are sand in the machinery of life; faith is the oil.

E. Stanley Jones

This life of faith, then, consists in just this—being a child in the Father's house. Let the ways of childish confidence and freedom from care, which so please you and win your heart when you observe your own little ones, teach you what you should be in your attitude toward God.

Hannah Whitall Smith

Today is the tomorrow we worried about yesterday.

Dennis Swanberg

A PRAYER FOR TODAY

Dear Lord, wherever I find myself, let me
celebrate more and worry less. When my faith
begins to waver, help me to trust You more.
Then, with praise on my lips and the love of
Your Son in my heart, let me live courageously,
faithfully, prayerfully, and thankfully
this day and every day. Amen

Today I Will Write Down My Thoughts About . . .

The things that I worry about, and the strength that I can,
and should, draw from God's promises.

_____

_____

_____

_____

_____

_____

_____

_____

_____

_____

_____

_____

_____

_____

_____

_____

THE POWER OF PERSEVERANCE

Let us not become weary in doing good,
for at the proper time we will reap a harvest
if we do not give up.
Galatians 6:9 NIV

Someone once said, "Life is a marathon, not a sprint." As you continue to search for purpose in everyday life (while, at the same time, balancing all your roles and responsibilities), you'll encounter your fair share of roadblocks and stumbling blocks. These situations require courage, patience, and above all, perseverance. As an example of perfect perseverance, you need look no further than your Savior, Jesus Christ.

Jesus, finished what He began. Despite the torture He endured, despite the shame of the cross, Jesus was steadfast in His faithfulness to God. We, too, must remain faithful, especially during times of hardship.

Are you tired? Ask God for strength. Are you discouraged? Believe in His promises. Are you frustrated or fearful? Pray as if everything depended upon God, and work as if everything depended upon you. With God's help, you will find the strength to be the kind of person who makes your Heavenly Father beam with pride.

Perhaps you are in a hurry for God to reveal His plans for your life. If so, be forewarned: God operates on His own timetable, not yours. Sometimes, God may answer your prayers with silence, and when He does, you must patiently persevere. In times of trouble, you must remain steadfast and trust in the merciful goodness of your Heavenly Father. Whatever your problem, He can handle it. Your job is to keep persevering until He does.

We ought to make some progress, however little, every day, and show some increase of fervor. We ought to act as if we were at war—as, indeed, we are—and never relax until we have won the victory.

St. Teresa of Avila

God never gives up on you, so don't you ever give up on Him.

Marie T. Freeman

God is bigger than your problems. Whatever worries press upon you today, put them in God's hands and leave them there.

Billy Graham

Success actually becomes a habit through the determined overcoming of obstacles as we meet them one by one.

Laura Ingalls Wilder

Stand still and refuse to retreat. Look at it as God looks at it and draw upon his power to hold up under the blast.

Charles Swindoll

Just remember, every flower that ever bloomed had to go through a whole lot of dirt to get there!

Barbara Johnson

MORE FROM GOD'S WORD ABOUT PERSEVERANCE

For you have need of endurance, so that when you have done the will of God, you may receive what was promised.

Hebrews 10:36 NASB

Thanks be to God! He gives us the victory through our Lord Jesus Christ. Therefore, my dear brothers, stand firm. Let nothing move you. Always give yourselves fully to the work of the Lord, because you know that your labor in the Lord is not in vain.

1 Corinthians 15:57-58 NIV

Be diligent that ye may be found of him in peace, without spot, and blameless.

2 Peter 3:14 KJV

It is better to finish something than to start it. It is better to be patient than to be proud.

Ecclesiastes 7:8 NCV

I have fought a good fight, I have finished my course, I have kept the faith.

2 Timothy 4:7 KJV

NEVER GIVE UP

Occasional disappointments, detours, and failures are inevitable, even for the most accomplished among us. Setbacks are simply the price that we must sometimes pay for our willingness to take risks as we follow our dreams. But when we encounter these hardships, we must never lose faith.

American children's rights advocate Marian Wright Edelman asked, "Whoever said anybody has a right to give up?" And that's a question that you most certainly should ask yourself, especially when times get tough.

Are you willing to keep fighting the good fight even when you meet unexpected difficulties? If you'll decide to press on through temporary setbacks, you may soon be surprised at the creative ways God finds to help determined people like you—people who possess the wisdom and the courage to persevere.

TODAY'S TIP

The world encourages instant gratification but God's work takes time: Remember the words of C. H. Spurgeon: "By perseverance, the snail reached the ark."

More Things to Think About

Achieving that goal is a good feeling, but to get there you have to also get through the failures. You've got to be able to pick yourself up and continue.

Mary Lou Retton

Failure is one of life's most powerful teachers. How we handle our failures determines whether we're going to simply "get by" in life or "press on."

Beth Moore

Jesus taught that perseverance is the essential element in prayer.

E. M. Bounds

That is the source of Jeremiah's living persistence, his creative constancy. He was up before the sun, listening to God's word. Rising early, he was quiet and attentive before his Lord. Long before the yelling started, the mocking, the complaining, there was this centering, discovering, exploring time with God.

Eugene Peterson

Press on. Obstacles are seldom the same size tomorrow as they are today.

Robert Schuller

A PRAYER FOR TODAY

Lord, when life is difficult, I am tempted to
abandon hope in the future. But You are
my God, and I can draw strength from You.
Let me trust You, Father, in good times
and in bad times. Let me persevere—
even if my soul is troubled—and let me follow
Your Son, Jesus Christ, this day and forever.
Amen

Today I Will Write Down My Thoughts About . . .

The need to keep working and the importance of perseverance.

_____

_____

_____

_____

_____

_____

_____

_____

_____

_____

_____

_____

_____

_____

_____

_____

_____

_____

TRUSTING GOD'S WORD

Heaven and earth will pass away,
but My words will never pass away.

Matthew 24:35 HCSB

God's promises are found in a book like no other: the Holy Bible. The Bible is a roadmap for life here on earth and for life eternal. As Christians, we are called upon to trust its promises, to follow its commandments, and to share its Good News.

As believers, we must study the Bible each day and meditate upon its meaning for our lives. Otherwise, we deprive ourselves of a priceless gift from our Creator. God's Holy Word is, indeed, a transforming, life-changing, one-of-a-kind treasure. And, a passing acquaintance with the Good Book is insufficient for Christians who seek to obey God's Word and to understand His will.

God has made promises to mankind and to you. God's promises never fail and they never grow old. You must trust those promises and share them with your family, with your friends, and with the world.

Are you standing on the promises of God? Are you expecting God to do wonderful things, or are you living beneath a cloud of apprehension and doubt? The familiar words of Psalm 118:24 remind us of a profound yet simple truth: "This is the day which the LORD hath made; we will rejoice and be glad in it" (KJV). Do you trust that promise, and do you live accordingly? If so, you are living the passionate life that God intends.

For passionate believers, every day begins and ends with God's Son and God's promises. When we accept Christ into our hearts, God promises us the opportunity for earthly peace and spiritual abundance. But more importantly, God promises us the priceless gift of eternal life.

As we face the inevitable challenges of life-here-on-earth, we must arm ourselves with the promises of God's Holy Word. When we do, we can expect the best, not only for the day ahead, but also for all eternity.

God's Word is a light not only to our path but also to our thinking. Place it in your heart today, and you will never walk in darkness.

Joni Eareckson Tada

Believe God's word and power more than you believe your own feelings and experiences.

Samuel Rutherford

I have found in the Bible words for my inmost thoughts, songs for my joy, utterance for my hidden griefs and pleadings for my shame and feebleness.

Samuel Taylor Coleridge

To say the Bible is infallible and inerrant is to declare that Scripture is totally trustworthy. Consequently, we must approach the text humbly and expectantly, open to being taught by the Spirit.

Stanley Grenz

If we are not continually fed with God's Word, we will starve spiritually.

Stormie Omartian

A thorough knowledge of the Bible is worth more than a college education.

Theodore Roosevelt

God did not write a book and send it by messenger to be read at a distance by unaided minds. He spoke a Book and lives in His spoken words, constantly speaking His words and causing the power of them to persist across the years.

A. W. Tozer

MORE FROM GOD'S WORD ABOUT GOD'S WORD

But the word of the Lord endures forever. And this is the word that was preached as the gospel to you.

1 Peter 1:25 HCSB

All Scripture is inspired by God and is profitable for teaching, for rebuking, for correcting, for training in righteousness, so that the man of God may be complete, equipped for every good work.

2 Timothy 3:16-17 HCSB

For the word of God is living and effective and sharper than any two-edged sword, penetrating as far as to divide soul, spirit, joints, and marrow; it is a judge of the ideas and thoughts of the heart.

Hebrews 4:12 HCSB

The one who is from God listens to God's words. This is why you don't listen, because you are not from God.

John 8:47 HCSB

The words of the Lord are pure words, like silver tried in a furnace . . . .

Psalm 12:6 NKJV

The Transforming Gift

The words of Matthew 4:4 remind us that, "Man shall not live by bread alone but by every word that proceedeth out of the mouth of God" (KJV). Have you established a passionate relationship with God's Holy Word? Hopefully so. After all, the Bible is a roadmap for life here on earth and for life eternal. And, as a believer who has been touched by God's grace, you are called upon to study God's Holy Word, to trust His Word, to follow its commandments, and to share its Good News with the world.

As believers, we must study the Bible and meditate upon its meaning for our lives. Otherwise, we deprive ourselves of a priceless gift from our Creator. God's Holy Word is, indeed, a transforming gift from the Father in heaven. That's why passionate believers must never live by bread alone . . .

Today's Tip

Trust God's Word: Charles Swindoll writes, "There are four words I wish we would never forget, and they are, 'God keeps His word.'" And remember: When it comes to studying God's Word, school is always in session.

More Things to Think About

Walking in faith brings you to the Word of God. There you will be healed, cleansed, fed, nurtured, equipped, and matured.

Kay Arthur

It is impossible to rightly govern the world without God and the Bible. Do not ever let anyone claim to be a true American patriot if they ever attempt to separate Religion from politics.

George Washington

The Scriptures were not given for our information, but for our transformation.

D. L. Moody

God's voice isn't all that difficult to hear. He sometimes shouts through our pain, whispers to us while we're relaxing on vacation, occasionally, He sings to us in a song, and warns us through the sixty-six books of His written Word. It's right there, ink on paper. Count on it—that book will never lead you astray.

Charles Swindoll

I believe the Bible is the best gift God has given to man.

Abraham Lincoln

A PRAYER FOR TODAY

Heavenly Father, Your Holy Word is a light
unto the world; let me study it, trust it,
and share it with all who cross my path.
In all that I do, help me be a worthy witness for
You as I share the Good News of Your perfect
Son and Your perfect Word. Amen

Today I Will Write Down My Thoughts About . . .

The need to allow God's Word to guide my path and shape my life.

_____

_____

_____

_____

_____

_____

_____

_____

_____

_____

_____

_____

_____

_____

_____

TRUST HIS POWER

Now faith is the substance of things hoped for, the evidence of things not seen.

Hebrews 11:1 KJV

We live in a world of infinite possibilities. But sometimes, because of limited faith and limited understanding, we wrongly assume that God cannot or will not intervene in the affairs of mankind. Such assumptions are simply wrong.

Are you afraid to ask God to do big things in your life? Is your faith threadbare and worn? If so, it's time to abandon your doubts and reclaim your faith—faith in yourself, faith in your abilities, faith in your future, and faith in your Heavenly Father.

Catherine Marshall notes that, "God specializes in things thought impossible." And make no mistake: God can help you do things you never dreamed possible . . . your job is to let Him.

Sometimes, when we read of God's miraculous works in Biblical times, we tell ourselves, "That was then, but this is now." When we do so, we are mistaken. God is with His children "now" just as He was "then." He is right here, right now, performing miracles. And, He will continue to work miracles in our lives to the extent we are willing to trust in Him and to the extent those miracles fit into the fabric of His divine plan.

Miracles—both great and small—happen around us all day every day, but usually, we're too busy to notice. Some miracles, like the twinkling of a star or the glory of a sunset, we take for granted. Other miracles, like the healing of a terminally sick patient, we chalk up to fate or to luck. We assume, quite incorrectly, that God is "out there" and we are "right here." Nothing could be farther from the truth.

Do you lack the faith that God can work miracles in your own life? If so, it's time to reconsider. Instead of doubting God, trust His power, and expect His miracles. Then, wait patiently…because something miraculous is about to happen.

Love is the seed of all hope.
It is the enticement to trust, to risk,
to try, and to go on.

Gloria Gaither

The essence of optimism is that it takes no account of the present, but it is a source of inspiration, of vitality, and of hope. Where others have resigned, it enables a man to hold his head high, to claim the future for himself, and not abandon it to his enemy.

Dietrich Bonhoeffer

You can look forward with hope, because one day there will be no more separation, no more scars, and no more suffering in My Father's House. It's the home of your dreams!

Anne Graham Lotz

And still today, when you boil it all down, our message to the world—even to the world that comes disguised as our child's schoolteacher, our next-door neighbor, or our personal hair stylist—is hope. Hope beyond the slavery of sin. And hope beyond the grave.

Becky Tirabassi

Without the certainty of His resurrection, we would come to the end of this life without hope, with nothing to anticipate except despair and doubt. But because He lives, we rejoice, knowing soon we will meet our Savior face to face, and the troubles and trials of this world will be behind us.

Bill Bright

MORE FROM GOD'S WORD ABOUT HOPE

Let us hold fast the confession of our hope without wavering, for He who promised is faithful.

Hebrews 10:23 NASB

I wait quietly before God, for my hope is in him.

Psalm 62:5 NLT

This hope we have as an anchor of the soul, a hope both sure and steadfast.

Hebrews 6:19 NASB

Full of hope, you'll relax, confident again; you'll look around, sit back, and take it easy.

Job 11:18 MSG

May the God of hope fill you with all joy and peace as you trust in him, so that you may overflow with hope by the power of the Holy Spirit.

Romans 15:13 NIV

HOPE IN CHRIST

Despite God's promises, despite Christ's love, and despite our countless blessings, we frail human beings can still lose hope from time to time. When we do, we need the encouragement of Christian friends, the life-changing power of prayer, and the healing truth of God's Holy Word. If we find ourselves falling into the spiritual traps of worry and discouragement, we should seek the healing touch of Jesus and the encouraging words of fellow Christians. Even though this world can be a place of trials and struggles, God has promised us peace, joy, and eternal life if we give ourselves to Him. And, of course, God keeps His promises today, tomorrow, and forever.

TODAY'S TIP

Don't give up hope: Other people have experienced the same kind of hard times you may be experiencing now. They made it, and so can you. (Psalm 146:5)

Many things are possible for
the person who has hope.
Even more is possible for
the person who has faith.
And still more is possible for
the person who knows
how to love.
But everything is possible for
the person who practices
all three virtues.

—

Brother Lawrence

MORE THINGS TO THINK ABOUT

Nothing in this world is more fundamental for success in life than hope, and this star pointed to our only source of true hope: Jesus Christ.

D. James Kennedy

Hope is the desire and the ability to move forward.

Emilie Barnes

The hope we have in Jesus is the anchor for the soul—something sure and steadfast, preventing drifting or giving way, lowered to the depth of God's love.

Franklin Graham

Oh, remember this: There is never a time when we may not hope in God. Whatever our necessities, however great our difficulties, and though to all appearance help is impossible, yet our business is to hope in God, and it will be found that it is not in vain.

George Mueller

Those who keep speaking about the sun while walking under a cloudy sky are messengers of hope, the true saints of our day.

Henri Nouwen

A Prayer for Today

Dear Lord, I will place my hope in You.
If I become discouraged, I will turn to You.
If I am afraid, I will seek strength in You.
In every aspect of my life, I will trust You.
You are my Father, and I will place my hope,
my trust, and my faith in You. Amen

Today I Will Write Down My Thoughts About . . .

The quality of my thoughts: Do I have hope for the future?
Do I really trust God's promises? Is my faith as strong as it
needs to be?

_____

_____

_____

_____

_____

_____

_____

_____

_____

_____

_____

_____

_____

_____

_____

TRUSTING GOD'S PLANS

And we know that in all things God works
for the good of those who love him,
who have been called according to his purpose.

Romans 8:28 NIV

D o you want to experience a life filled with abundance and peace? If so, here's a word of warning: you'll need to resist the temptation to do things "your way" and commit, instead, to do things God's way.

God has plans for your life. Big plans. But He won't force you to follow His will; to the contrary, He has given you free will, the ability to make decisions on your own. With the freedom to choose comes the responsibility of living with the consequences of the choices you make.

The most important decision of your life is, of course, your commitment to accept Jesus Christ as your personal Lord and Savior. And once your eternal destiny is secured, you will undoubtedly ask yourself the question "What now, Lord?" If you earnestly seek God's will for your life, you will find it . . . in time.

When you make the decision to seek God's will for your life, you will contemplate His Word, and you will be watchful for His signs. You will associate with fellow believers who will encourage your spiritual growth. And, you will listen to that inner voice that speaks to you in the quiet moments of your daily devotionals.

Sometimes, God's plans are crystal clear, but other times, He leads you through the wilderness before He delivers you to the Promised Land. So be patient, keep searching, and keep praying. If you do, then in time, God will answer your prayers and make His plans known.

God is right here, and He intends to use you in wonderful, unexpected ways. You'll discover those plans by doing things His way . . . and you'll be eternally grateful that you did.

We are uncertain of the next step,
but we are certain of God.

Oswald Chambers

I'm convinced that there is nothing that can happen to
me in this life that is not precisely designed by a sovereign
Lord to give me the opportunity to learn to know Him.

Elisabeth Elliot

There is something incredibly comforting about knowing
that the Creator is in control of your life.

Lisa Whelchel

God specializes in things fresh and firsthand. His plans for
you this year may outshine those of the past. He's prepared
to fill your days with reasons to give Him praise.

Joni Eareckson Tada

In those desperate times when we feel like we don't have
an ounce of strength, He will gently pick up our heads so
that our eyes can behold something—something that will
keep His hope alive in us.

Kathy Troccoli

In God's plan, God is the standard for perfection. We
don't compare ourselves to others; they are just as fouled
up as we are. The goal is to be like him; anything less is
inadequate.

Max Lucado

With God, it's never "Plan B"
or "second best." It's always
"Plan A." And, if we let Him,
He'll make something
beautiful of our lives.

—

Gloria Gaither

MORE FROM GOD'S WORD ABOUT GOD'S PLAN

Teach me Your way, O Lord; I will walk in Your truth.

Psalm 86:11 NKJV

The Lord shatters the plans of nations and thwarts all their schemes. But the Lord's plans stand firm forever; his intentions can never be shaken.

Psalm 33:10-11 NLT

Trust the Lord your God with all your heart and lean not on your own understanding; in all your ways acknowledge him, and he will make your paths straight.

Proverbs 3:5-6 NIV

There is one thing I always do. Forgetting the past and straining toward what is ahead, I keep trying to reach the goal and get the prize for which God called me . . . .

Philippians 3:13–14 NCV

"I say this because I know what I am planning for you," says the Lord. "I have good plans for you, not plans to hurt you. I will give you hope and a good future."

Jeremiah 29:11 NCV

VERY BIG PLANS

All of us must, from time to time, endure days filled with suffering and pain. And as human beings with limited understanding, we can never fully understand the plans of our Father in heaven. But we must learn to trust Him.

Corrie ten Boom understood that her own ability to understand the ebbs and flows of life was limited—but that God's is not. She said, "O Lord, thank You that Your side of the embroidery of our life is always perfect. That is such a comfort when our side is sometimes so mixed up."

From time to time, you, like Corrie, will face trials and tribulations. And you may ask "Why me?" But even on life's darker days, you should be comforted by the knowledge that God is in charge, and that He has plans for you . . . very big plans.

TODAY'S TIP

God has a wonderful plan for your life. And the time to start looking for that plan—and living it—is now. Discovering God's plan begins with prayer, but it doesn't end there. You've also got to work at it.

MORE THINGS TO THINK ABOUT

If we stay with the Lord, enduring to the end of His great plan for us, we will enjoy the rest that results from living in the kingdom of God.

Serita Ann Jakes

We forget that God sometimes has to say "No." We pray to Him as our heavenly Father, and like wise human fathers, He often says, "No," not from whim or caprice, but from wisdom, from love, and from knowing what is best for us.

Peter Marshall

The secret you stumble on is this: If, once hurt, you open your heart and let God take you by the hand, he will lead you to a better place than you have known.

Paula Rinehart

We must be willing to give up every dream but God's dream.

Larry Crabb

It is easy to determine the importance money plays in God's plan by the abundance of Scripture that relates to it—more than seven hundred verses directly refer to its use.

Larry Burkett

A Prayer for Today

Dear Lord, I will earnestly seek Your will for
my life. You have a plan for me that I can never
fully understand. But You understand.
And I will trust You today, tomorrow,
and forever. Amen

Today I Will Write Down My Thoughts About . . .

Some of the things that I believe God wants me to do with
my life during the coming year.

_____

_____

_____

_____

_____

_____

_____

_____

_____

_____

_____

_____

_____

_____

_____

_____

_____

HE RENEWS
YOUR STRENGTH

*The One who was sitting on the throne said,
"Look! I am making everything new!"
Then he said, "Write this, because these words
are true and can be trusted."*

Revelation 21:5 NCV

E ven the most inspired Christians can, from time to time, find themselves running on empty. The demands of daily life can drain us of our strength and rob us of the joy that is rightfully ours in Christ. When we find ourselves tired, discouraged, or worse, there is a source from which we can draw the power needed to recharge our spiritual batteries. That source is God.

God intends that His children lead joyous lives filled with abundance and peace. But sometimes, abundance and peace seem very far away. It is then that we must turn to God for renewal, and when we do, He will restore us.

Are you tired or troubled? Turn your heart toward God in prayer. Are you weak or worried? Take the time—or, more accurately, make the time—to delve deeply into God's Holy Word. Are you spiritually depleted? Call upon fellow believers to support you, and call upon Christ to renew your spirit and your life. When you do, you'll discover that the Creator of the universe stands always ready and always able to create a new sense of wonderment and joy in you.

The well of God's forgiveness never runs dry.

Grady Nutt

Repentance removes old sins and wrong attitudes, and it opens the way for the Holy Spirit to restore our spiritual health.

Shirley Dobson

He is the God of wholeness and restoration.

Stormie Omartian

God gives us permission to forget our past and the understanding to live our present. He said He will remember our sins no more. (Psalm 103:11-12)

Serita Ann Jakes

Christ came when all things were growing old. He made them new.

St. Augustine

Resolutely slam and lock the door on past sin and failure, and throw away the key.

Oswald Chambers

Walking with God leads to receiving his intimate counsel, and counseling leads to deep restoration.

John Eldredge

God uses ordinary people who
are obedient to Him to do
extraordinary things.

—

John Maxwell

MORE FROM GOD'S WORD ABOUT RENEWAL

When doubts filled my mind, your comfort gave me renewed hope and cheer.

Psalm 94:19 NLT

Create in me a pure heart, O God, and renew a steadfast spirit within me. Do not cast me from your presence or take your Holy Spirit from me. Restore to me the joy of your salvation and grant me a willing spirit, to sustain me.

Psalm 51:10-12 NIV

He makes me to lie down in green pastures; He leads me beside the still waters. He restores my soul; He leads me in the paths of righteousness for His name's sake.

Psalm 23:2–3 NKJV

Come to Me, all you who labor and are heavy laden, and I will give you rest. Take My yoke upon you and learn from Me, for I am gentle and lowly in heart, and you will find rest for your souls. For My yoke is easy and My burden is light.

Matthew 11:28-30 NKJV

But those who wait on the Lord shall renew their strength; they shall mount up with wings like eagles, they shall run and not be weary, they shall walk and not faint.

Isaiah 40:31 NKJV

HIS WORK, HIS STRENGTH

Today, like every other day, is literally brimming with possibilities. Whether we realize it or not, God is always working in us and through us; our job is to let Him do His work without undue interference. Yet we are imperfect beings who, because of our limited vision, often resist God's will. We want life to unfold according to our own desires, not God's. But, our Heavenly Father may have other plans.

As you begin this day, think carefully about the work that God can do through you. And then, set out upon the next phase of your life's journey with a renewed sense of purpose and hope. God has the power to make all things new, including you. Your job is to let Him do it.

TODAY'S TIP

Do you need time for yourself? Take it. Ruth Bell Graham observed, "It is important that we take time out for ourselves—for relaxation, for refreshment." Enough said.

More Things to Think About

But while relaxation is one thing, refreshment is another. We need to drink frequently and at length from God's fresh springs, to spend time in the Scripture, time in fellowship with Him, time worshiping Him.

Ruth Bell Graham

When we reach the end of our strength, wisdom, and personal resources, we enter into the beginning of his glorious provisions.

Patsy Clairmont

Each of us has something broken in our lives: a broken promise, a broken dream, a broken marriage, a broken heart . . . and we must decide how we're going to deal with our brokenness. We can wallow in self-pity or regret, accomplishing nothing and having no fun or joy in our circumstances; or we can determine with our will to take a few risks, get out of our comfort zone, and see what God will do to bring unexpected delight in our time of need.

Luci Swindoll

One reason so much American Christianity is a mile wide and an inch deep is that Christians are simply tired. Sometimes you need to kick back and rest for Jesus' sake.

Dennis Swanberg

A PRAYER FOR TODAY

Dear Lord, sometimes I grow weary;
sometimes I am discouraged;
sometimes I am fearful. Yet when I turn
my heart and my prayers to You, I am secure.
Renew my strength, Father, and let me draw
comfort and courage from Your promises and
from Your unending love. Amen

Today I Will Write Down My Thoughts About . . .

The strength that is mine when I follow God's path and trust His promises.

_____

_____

_____

_____

_____

_____

_____

_____

_____

_____

_____

_____

_____

_____

_____

_____

_____

_____

BEYOND DOUBT

If you don't know what you're doing,
pray to the Father. He loves to help. You'll get
his help, and won't be condescended to when you
ask for it. Ask boldly, believingly, without a second
thought. People who "worry their prayers" are like
wind-whipped waves. Don't think you're going to
get anything from the Master that way, adrift at sea,
keeping all your options open.

James 1:5-8 MSG

Doubts come in several shapes and sizes: doubts about God, doubts about the future, and doubts about your own abilities, for starters. And what, precisely, does God's Word say in response to these doubts? The Bible is clear: when we are beset by doubts, of whatever kind, we must draw ourselves nearer to God through worship and through prayer. When we do so, God, the loving Father who has never left our sides, draws ever closer to us (James 4:8).

In the book of Matthew, we are told of a terrible storm that rose quickly on the Sea of Galilee while Jesus and His disciples were in a boat, far from shore. The disciples were filled with fear. Although they had witnessed many miracles firsthand—although they had walked and talked with Him—the disciples were still filled with doubts. So they cried out to their Master, and Christ responded, "Why are you fearful, O you of little faith?" Then He arose and rebuked the winds and the sea, and there was a great calm. So the men marveled, saying, "Who can this be, that even the winds and the sea obey Him?" (Matthew 8:26-27 NKJV).

Sometimes, like Jesus' disciples, we feel threatened by the storms of life. Sometimes we may feel distant from God; sometimes we may question His power or His plans. During these moments, when our hearts are flooded with uncertainty, we must remember that God is not simply near, He is here.

Have you ever felt your faith in God slipping away? If so, you are not alone. Every life—including yours—is a series of successes and failures, celebrations and disappointments, joys and sorrows, hopes and doubts. Even the most faithful Christians are overcome by occasional bouts of fear and doubt, and so, too, will you. But even when you feel far removed from God, God never leaves your side, not for an instant. He is always with you, always willing to calm the storms of life. When you sincerely seek His presence—and when you genuinely seek to establish a deeper, more meaningful relationship with His Son—God is prepared to touch your heart, to calm your fears, to answer your doubts, and to restore our soul.

I have found the perfect antidote for fear.
Whenever it sticks up its ugly face,
I clobber it with prayer.

Dale Evans Rogers

Seldom do you enjoy the luxury of making decisions that are based on enough evidence to absolutely silence all skepticism.

Bill Hybels

To wrestle with God does not mean that we have lost faith, but that we are fighting for it.

Sheila Walsh

In our constant struggle to believe, we are likely to overlook the simple fact that a bit of healthy disbelief is sometimes as needful as faith to the welfare of our souls.

A. W. Tozer

We basically have two choices to make in dealing with the mysteries of God. We can wrestle with Him or we can rest in Him.

Calvin Miller

I was learning something important: we are most vulnerable to the piercing winds of doubt when we distance ourselves from the mission and fellowship to which Christ has called us. Our night of discouragement will seem endless and our task impossible, unless we recognize that He stands in our midst.

Joni Eareckson Tada

MORE FROM GOD'S WORD ABOUT DOUBT

Purify your hearts, ye double-minded.

James 4:8 KJV

*Immediately the father of the child cried out and said with tears,
"Lord, I believe; help my unbelief!"*

Mark 9:24 NKJV

*So He said, "Come." And when Peter had come down out of
the boat, he walked on the water to go to Jesus. But when he
saw that the wind was boisterous, he was afraid; and beginning
to sink he cried out, saying, "Lord, save me!" And immediately
Jesus stretched out His hand and caught him, and said to him,
"O you of little faith, why did you doubt?" And when they got
into the boat, the wind ceased.*

Matthew 14:29-32 NKJV

*When doubts filled my mind, your comfort gave me renewed
hope and cheer.*

Psalm 94:19 NLT

*Jesus said, "Because you have seen Me, you have believed.
Blessed are those who believe without seeing."*

John 20:29 HCSB

Above and Beyond Fear

We live in a fear-based world, a world where bad news travels at light speed and good news doesn't. These are troubled times, times when we have legitimate fears for the future of our nation, our world, and our families. But as Christians, we have every reason to live courageously. After all, the ultimate battle has already been fought and won on that faraway cross at Calvary.

Perhaps you, like countless other believers, have found your courage tested by the anxieties and fears that are an inevitable part of 21st-century life. If so, God wants to have a little chat with you. The next time you find your courage tested to the limit, God wants to remind you that He is not just near; He is here.

Your Heavenly Father is your Protector and your Deliverer. Call upon Him in your hour of need, and be comforted. Whatever your challenge, whatever your trouble, God can handle it. And will.

Today's Tip

Doubts creeping in? Increase the amount of time you spend in Bible Study, prayer, and worship.

MORE THINGS TO THINK ABOUT

Fear is a self-imposed prison that will keep you from becoming what God intends for you to be.

Rick Warren

When we meditate on God and remember the promises He has given us in His Word, our faith grows, and our fears dissolve.

Charles Stanley

The Bible is a Christian's guidebook, and I believe the knowledge it sheds on pain and suffering is the great antidote to fear for suffering people. Knowledge can dissolve fear as light destroys darkness.

Philip Yancey

God shields us from most of the things we fear, but when He chooses not to shield us, He unfailingly allots grace in the measure needed.

Elisabeth Elliot

Only believe, don't fear. Our Master, Jesus, always watches over us, and no matter what the persecution, Jesus will surely overcome it.

Lottie Moon

A PRAYER FOR TODAY

Dear Lord, when I am filled with uncertainty and doubt, give me faith. In the dark moments of life, keep me mindful of Your healing power and Your infinite love, so that I may live courageously and faithfully today and every day.

Amen

Today I Will Write Down My Thoughts About . . .

The size of the things I fear in contrast to the size of God's power.

_____

_____

_____

_____

_____

_____

_____

_____

_____

_____

_____

_____

_____

_____

_____

SENSING GOD'S PRESENCE

*You will seek Me and find Me
when you search for Me with all your heart.*
Jeremiah 29:13 HCSB

In the quiet early morning, as the sun's first rays stream over the horizon, we may sense the presence of God. But as the day wears on and the demands of everyday life bear down upon us, we may become so wrapped up in earthly concerns that we forget to praise the Creator.

God is everywhere we have ever been and everywhere we will ever be. When we turn to Him often, we are blessed by His presence. But, if we ignore God's presence or rebel against it altogether, the world in which we live soon becomes a spiritual wasteland.

Since God is everywhere, we are free to sense His presence whenever we take the time to quiet our souls and turn our prayers to Him. But sometimes, amid the incessant demands of everyday life, we turn our thoughts far from God; when we do, we suffer.

Do you set aside quiet moments each day to offer praise to your Creator? You should. During these moments of stillness, you can sense the infinite love and power of our Lord. The familiar words of Psalm 46:10 remind us to "Be still, and know that I am God" (KJV). When we do so, we encounter the awesome presence of our loving Heavenly Father.

Are you tired, discouraged, or fearful? Be comforted because God is with you. Are you confused? Listen to the quiet voice of your Heavenly Father. Are you bitter? Talk with God and seek His guidance. Are you celebrating a great victory? Thank God and praise Him. He is the

Giver of all things good. In whatever condition you find yourself—whether you are happy or sad, victorious or vanquished, troubled or triumphant—celebrate God's presence. And be comforted in the knowledge that God is not just near. He is here.

God is sort of like the wind
in that we see evidence of His presence;
yet He isn't easily grasped.

Patsy Clairmont

If you want to hear God's voice clearly and you are uncertain, then remain in His presence until He changes that uncertainty. Often, much can happen during this waiting for the Lord. Sometimes, He changes pride into humility, doubt into faith and peace.

Corrie ten Boom

Make the least of all that goes and the most of all that comes. Don't regret what is past. Cherish what you have. Look forward to all that is to come. And most important of all, rely moment by moment on Jesus Christ.

Gigi Graham Tchividjian

God walks with us. He scoops us up in His arms or simply sits with us in silent strength until we cannot avoid the awesome recognition that yes, even now, He is here.

Gloria Gaither

In the sanctuary, we discover beauty: the beauty of His presence.

Kay Arthur

Sometimes the loveliness of God's presence comes in the midst of pain.

Madeleine L'Engle

MORE FROM GOD'S WORD ABOUT GOD'S PRESENCE

The Lord is near all who call out to Him, all who call out to Him with integrity. He fulfills the desires of those who fear Him; He hears their cry for help and saves them.

Psalm 145:18-19 HCSB

Surely goodness and mercy shall follow me all the days of my life: and I will dwell in the house of the Lord for ever.

Psalm 23:6 KJV

I am not alone, because the Father is with Me.

John 16:32 HCSB

Again, this is God's command: to believe in his personally named Son, Jesus Christ. He told us to love each other, in line with the original command. As we keep his commands, we live deeply and surely in him, and he lives in us. And this is how we experience his deep and abiding presence in us: by the Spirit he gave us.

1 John 3:23-24 MSG

For the eyes of the Lord range throughout the earth to strengthen those whose hearts are fully committed to him.

2 Chronicles 16:9 NIV

HE'S ALWAYS THERE

God promises that He is with us wherever we go. He is never absent from our lives or from our world; to the contrary, God's hand is actively involved in the smallest details of everyday life. He is not somewhere "out there"; He is "right here, right now," continuously reshaping His creation.

God is with you always, listening to your thoughts and prayers, watching your every step. As the demands of life weigh down upon you, you may be tempted to ignore God's presence. But, when you quiet yourself and acknowledge His presence, God will touch your heart and restore your spirits.

At this very moment, God is seeking to work in you and through you. Are you willing to let Him?

TODAY'S TIP

Having trouble hearing God? If so, slow yourself down, tune out the distractions, and listen carefully. God has important things to say; your task is to be still and listen.

MORE THINGS TO THINK ABOUT

The Lord Jesus by His Holy Spirit is with me, and the knowledge of His presence dispels the darkness and allays any fears.

Bill Bright

The Bible teaches that God is an "everywhere-present" God.

Bill Hybels

God expresses His love toward us by His uninterrupted presence in our lives.

Charles Stanley

When we are in the presence of God, removed from distractions, we are able to hear him more clearly, and a secure environment has been established for the young and broken places in our hearts to surface.

John Eldredge

I have a capacity in my soul for taking in God entirely. I am as sure as I live that nothing is so near to me as God. God is nearer to me than I am to myself; my existence depends on the nearness and the presence of God.

Meister Eckhart

A PRAYER FOR TODAY

Dear Lord, You are with me when
I am strong and when I am weak.
You never leave my side, even when it seems
to me that You are far away.
Today and every day, let me trust
Your promises and let me feel Your love.
Amen

Today I Will Write Down My Thoughts About . . .

The importance of gaining strength, wisdom, and spiritual maturity by spending quiet moments with God.

_____

_____

_____

_____

_____

_____

_____

_____

_____

_____

_____

_____

_____

_____

_____

LEARNING THE ART OF ACCEPTANCE

He is the Lord. Let him do what he thinks is best.
1 Samuel 3:18 NCV

I f you're like most people, you like being in control. Period. You want things to happen according to your wishes and according to your timetable. But sometimes, God has other plans . . . and He always has the final word.

The American theologian Reinhold Niebuhr composed a profoundly simple verse that came to be known as the Serenity Prayer: "God, grant me the serenity to accept the things I cannot change, the courage to change the things I can, and the wisdom to know the difference." Niebuhr's words are far easier to recite than they are to live by.

Oswald Chambers correctly observed, "Our Lord never asks us to decide for Him; He asks us to yield to Him—a very different matter." These words remind us that even when we cannot understand the workings of God, we must trust Him and accept His will.

All of us experience adversity and pain. As human beings with limited comprehension, we can never fully understand the will of our Father in heaven. But as believers in a benevolent God, we must always trust His providence.

When Jesus went to the Mount of Olives, as described in Luke 22, He poured out His heart to God. Jesus knew of the agony that He was destined to endure, but He also knew that God's will must be done. We, like our Savior, face trials that bring fear and trembling to the very depths of our souls, but like Christ, we too must ultimately seek God's will, not our own.

Are you embittered by a personal tragedy that you did not deserve and cannot understand? If so, it's time to make peace with life. It's time to forgive others, and, if necessary, to forgive yourself. It's time to accept the unchangeable past, to embrace the priceless present, and to have faith in the promise of tomorrow. It's time to trust God completely. And it's time to reclaim the peace—His peace—that can and should be yours.

So if you've encountered unfortunate circumstances that are beyond your power to control, accept those circumstances . . . and trust God. When you do, you can be comforted in the knowledge that your Creator is both loving and wise, and that He understands His plans perfectly, even when you do not.

Loving Him means the thankful acceptance of
all things that His love has appointed.

Elisabeth Elliot

Have courage for the great sorrows of life and patience for the small ones; and when you have laboriously accomplished your daily task, go to sleep in peace. God is awake.

Victor Hugo

What cannot be altered must be borne, not blamed.

Thomas Fuller

Our Lord never asks us to decide for Him; He asks us to yield to Him—a very different matter.

Oswald Chambers

Our battles are first won or lost in the secret places of our will in God's presence, never in full view of the world.

Oswald Chambers

The key to contentment is to consider. Consider who you are and be satisfied with that. Consider what you have and be satisfied with that. Consider what God's doing and be satisfied with that.

Luci Swindoll

The more comfortable we are with mystery in our journey, the more rest we will know along the way.

John Eldredge

I am truly grateful that faith
enables me to move past
the question of "Why?"

—

Zig Ziglar

More from God's Word About Acceptance

A man's heart plans his way, but the Lord determines his steps.

Proverbs 16:9 HCSB

For everything created by God is good, and nothing should be rejected if it is received with thanksgiving.

1 Timothy 4:4 HCSB

Should we accept only good from God and not adversity?

Job 2:10 HCSB

Come to terms with God and be at peace; in this way good will come to you.

Job 22:21 HCSB

The Lord says, "Forget what happened before, and do not think about the past. Look at the new thing I am going to do. It is already happening. Don't you see it? I will make a road in the desert and rivers in the dry land."

Isaiah 43:18-19 NCV

BEYOND COMPREHENSION

Are you embittered by a personal tragedy that you did not deserve and cannot understand? If so, it's time to accept the unchangeable past and to have faith in the promise of tomorrow. It's time to trust God completely—and it's time to reclaim the peace—His peace—that can and should be yours.

On occasion, you will be confronted with situations that you simply don't understand. But God does. And He has a reason for everything that He does.

God doesn't explain Himself in ways that we, as mortals with limited insight and clouded vision, can comprehend. So, instead of understanding every aspect of God's unfolding plan for our lives and our universe, we must be satisfied to trust Him completely. We cannot know God's motivations, nor can we understand His actions. We can, however, trust Him, and we must.

TODAY'S TIP

Acceptance means learning to trust God more. Today, think of at least one aspect of your life that you've been reluctant to accept, and then prayerfully ask God to help you trust Him more by accepting the past.

More Things to Think About

In the kingdom of God, the surest way to lose something is to try to protect it, and the best way to keep it is to let it go.

A. W. Tozer

The one true way of dying to self is the way of patience, meekness, humility, and resignation to God.

Andrew Murray

When we face an impossible situation, all self-reliance and self-confidence must melt away; we must be totally dependent on Him for the resources.

Anne Graham Lotz

Acceptance says: True, this is my situation at the moment. I'll look unblinkingly at the reality of it. But, I'll also open my hands to accept willingly whatever a loving Father sends me.

Catherine Marshall

I have held many things in my hands, and I have lost them all; but whatever I have placed in God's hands, that I still possess.

Corrie ten Boom

A PRAYER FOR TODAY

Father, the events of this world unfold according
to a plan that I cannot fully understand.
But You understand. Help me to trust You,
Lord, even when I am grieving. Help me to trust
You even when I am confused. Today,
in whatever circumstances I find myself,
let me trust Your will and accept Your love . . .
completely. Amen

Today I Will Write Down My Thoughts About . . .

The troubling events in my past that I have not yet fully accepted; the events in my past that I should turn over to God—once and for all—and be done with.

_____

_____

_____

_____

_____

_____

_____

_____

_____

_____

_____

_____

_____

_____

_____

MAKING WORSHIP A HIGH PRIORITY

Worship the Lord your God and . . .
serve Him only.
Matthew 4:10 HCSB

All of humanity is engaged in worship. The question is not whether we worship, but what we worship. Wise men and women choose to worship God. When they do, they are blessed with a plentiful harvest of joy, peace, and abundance. Other people choose to distance themselves from God by foolishly worshiping things that are intended to bring personal gratification but not spiritual gratification. Such choices often have tragic consequences.

If we place our love for material possessions above our love for God—or if we yield to the countless temptations of this world—we find ourselves engaged in a struggle between good and evil, a clash between God and Satan. Our responses to these struggles have implications that echo throughout our families and throughout our communities.

How can we ensure that we cast our lot with God? We do so, in part, by the practice of regular, purposeful worship in the company of fellow believers. When we worship God faithfully and fervently, we are blessed. When we fail to worship God, for whatever reason, we forfeit the spiritual gifts that He intends for us.

We must worship our Heavenly Father, not just with our words, but also with deeds. We must honor Him, praise Him, and obey Him. As we seek to find purpose and meaning for our lives, we must first seek His purpose and His will. For believers, God comes first. Always first.

Do you place a high value on the practice of worship? Hopefully so. After all, every day provides countless opportunities to put God where He belongs: at the very center of your life. It's up to you to worship God seven days a week; anything less is simply not enough.

Worship is not taught from the pulpit.
It must be learned in the heart.

Jim Elliot

Worship at its core is a giving to God of all that is your best. This cannot be done without the sacrifice of the acclaim and adulation of the world.

Ravi Zacharias

Worship and worry cannot live in the same heart; they are mutually exclusive.

Ruth Bell Graham

In the sanctuary, we discover beauty: the beauty of His presence.

Kay Arthur

God asks that we worship Him with our concentrated minds as well as with our wills and emotions. A divided and scattered mind is not effective.

Catherine Marshall

Inside the human heart is an undeniable, spiritual instinct to commune with its Creator.

Jim Cymbala

Ultimately things work out best for those who make the best of the way things work out.

Barbara Johnson

Worship always empowers
the worshiper with
a greater revelation of
the object of her desire.

—

Lisa Bevere

MORE FROM GOD'S WORD ABOUT WORSHIP

God lifted him high and honored him far beyond anyone or anything, ever, so that all created beings in heaven and earth, even those long ago dead and buried, will bow in worship before this Jesus Christ, and call out in praise that he is the Master of all, to the glorious honor of God the Father.

Philippians 2:9-11 MSG

Worship the Lord with gladness. Come before him, singing with joy. Acknowledge that the Lord is God! He made us, and we are his. We are his people, the sheep of his pasture.

Psalm 100:2-3 NLT

A time is coming and has now come when the true worshipers will worship the Father in spirit and truth, for they are the kind of worshipers the Father seeks. God is spirit, and his worshipers must worship in spirit and in truth.

John 4:23-24 NIV

Blessed are they which do hunger and thirst after righteousness: for they shall be filled.

Matthew 5:6 KJV

Happy are those who hear the joyful call to worship, for they will walk in the light of your presence, Lord.

Psalm 89:15 NLT

THE HOUSE OF WORSHIP

Where do we worship? In our hearts or in our church? The answer is both. As Christians who have been saved by a loving, compassionate Creator, we are compelled not only to worship the Creator in our hearts but also to worship Him in the presence of fellow believers.

We live in a world that is teeming with temptations and distractions—a world where good and evil struggle in a constant battle to win our hearts and souls. Our challenge, of course, is to ensure that we cast our lot on the side of God. One way to ensure that we do so is by the practice of regular, purposeful worship with our families. When we worship God faithfully and fervently, we are blessed.

TODAY'S TIP

Worship reminds you of the awesome power of God. So worship Him daily, and allow Him to work through you every day of the week (not just on Sundays).

MORE THINGS TO THINK ABOUT

To worship is to quicken the conscience by the holiness of God, to feed the mind with the truth of God, to open the heart to the love of God, to devote the will to the purpose of God.

William Temple

You were Lord of the heavens before time was time, and Lord of all lords You will be! We bow down and we worship You, Lord.

Twila Paris

When God is at the center of your life, you worship. When he's not, you worry.

Rick Warren

Worship is our response to the overtures of love from the heart of the Father.

Richard Foster

Because his spiritual existence transcends form, matter, and location, we have the freedom to worship him and experience his indwelling presence wherever we are.

R. C. Sproul

A Prayer for Today

Lord, when I slow down and take the time to
worship You, my soul is blessed. Let me worship
You every day of my life, and let me discover
the peace that can be mine when
I welcome You into my heart. Amen

Today I Will Write Down My Thoughts About . . .

The role that worship currently plays in my life and the
role that it should play.

_____

_____

_____

_____

_____

_____

_____

_____

_____

_____

_____

_____

_____

_____

_____

CELEBRATING THE GIFT OF LIFE

This is the day the LORD has made;
let us rejoice and be glad in it.

Psalm 118:24 NIV

Today is a non-renewable resource—once it's gone, it's gone forever. Our responsibility, as thoughtful believers, is to use this day in the service of God's will and in the service of His people. When we do so, we enrich our own lives and the lives of those whom we love.

God has richly blessed us, and He wants you to rejoice in His gifts. That's why this day—and each day that follows—should be a time of prayer and celebration as we consider the Good News of God's free gift: salvation through Jesus Christ.

Oswald Chambers correctly observed, "Joy is the great note all throughout the Bible." E. Stanley Jones echoed that thought when he wrote "Christ and joy go together." But, even the most dedicated Christians can, on occasion, forget to celebrate each day for what it is: a priceless gift from God.

What do you expect from the day ahead? Are you expecting God to do wonderful things, or are you living beneath a cloud of apprehension and doubt? The familiar words of Psalm 118:24 remind us of a profound yet simple truth: "This is the day which the LORD hath made" (KJV). Our duty, as believers, is to rejoice in God's marvelous creation.

When we wholeheartedly commit ourselves to God, there is nothing mediocre or run-of-the-mill about us. To live for Christ is to be passionate about our Lord and about our lives.

—

Jim Gallery

If you can forgive the person you were, accept the person you are, and believe in the person you will become, you are headed for joy. So celebrate your life.

Barbara Johnson

A life of intimacy with God is characterized by joy.

Oswald Chambers

Joy is the direct result of having God's perspective on our daily lives and the effect of loving our Lord enough to obey His commands and trust His promises.

Bill Bright

I am truly happy with Jesus Christ. I couldn't live without Him.

Ruth Bell Graham

Christ is the secret, the source, the substance, the center, and the circumference of all true and lasting gladness.

Mrs. Charles E. Cowman

A joyful heart is like a sunshine of God's love, the hope of eternal happiness, a burning flame of God . . . . And if we pray, we will become that sunshine of God's love—in our own home, the place where we live, and in the world at large.

Mother Teresa

MORE FROM GOD'S WORD ABOUT CELEBRATION

So now we can rejoice in our wonderful new relationship with God—all because of what our Lord Jesus Christ has done for us in making us friends of God.

Romans 5:11 NLT

At the dedication of the wall of Jerusalem, the Levites were sought out from where they lived and were brought to Jerusalem to celebrate joyfully the dedication with songs of thanksgiving and with the music of cymbals, harps and lyres.

Nehemiah 12:27 NIV

A happy heart is like a continual feast.

Proverbs 15:15 NCV

Shout for joy to the LORD, all the earth. Worship the LORD with gladness; come before him with joyful songs.

Psalm 100:1-2 NIV

Rejoice in the Lord, you righteous ones; praise from the upright is beautiful.

Psalm 33:1 HCSB

Let the Celebration Begin

Life should never be taken for granted. Each day is a priceless gift from God and should be treated as such.

Hannah Whitall Smith observed, "How changed our lives would be if we could only fly through the days on wings of surrender and trust!" And Clement of Alexandria noted, "All our life is a celebration for us; we are convinced, in fact, that God is always everywhere. We sing while we work . . . we pray while we carry out all life's other occupations." These words remind us that this day is God's creation, a gift to be treasured and savored.

Today, let us celebrate life with smiles on our faces and kind words on our lips. After all, this is God's day, and He has given us clear instructions for its use. We are commanded to rejoice and be glad. So, with no further ado, let the celebration begin . . .

Today's Tip

God has given you the gift of life (here on earth) and the promise of eternal life (in heaven). Now, He wants you to celebrate those gifts. By celebrating the gift of life, you protect your heart from the dangers of pessimism, regret, hopelessness, and bitterness.

Celebration is possible only
through the deep realization that
life and death are never found
completely separate.
Celebration can really come
about only where fear and love,
joy and sorrow, tear and smiles
can exist together.

—

Henri Nouwen

More Things to Think About

Not every day of our lives is overflowing with joy and celebration. But there are moments when our hearts nearly burst within us for the sheer joy of being alive. The first sight of our newborn babies, the warmth of love in another's eyes, the fresh scent of rain on a hot summer's eve—moments like these renew in us a heartfelt appreciation for life.

Gwen Ellis

Some of us seem so anxious about avoiding hell that we forget to celebrate our journey toward heaven.

Philip Yancey

The church is the last place on earth to be solemn . . . provided you have lived right.

Sam Jones

I know nothing, except what everyone knows—if there when God dances, I should dance.

W. H. Auden

A PRAYER FOR TODAY

Dear Lord, today, I will join in the celebration of
life. I will be a joyful Christian, and I will share
my joy with all those who cross my path.
You have given me countless blessings, Lord,
and today I will thank You by celebrating
my life, my faith, and my Savior.
Amen

Today I Will Write Down My Thoughts About . . .

The need to celebrate God's gifts.

_____

_____

_____

_____

_____

_____

_____

_____

_____

_____

_____

_____

_____

_____

_____

_____

Worship is about rekindling
an ashen heart
into a blazing fire.

—

Liz Curtis Higgs